AN IDENTIFICATION GUIDE TO

MUSHROOMS OF BRITAIN

AND NORTHERN EUROPE

JOSEPHINE BACON

JOHN BEAUFOY PUBLISHING

Reprinted in 2024

This edition published in the United Kingdom in 2020 by John Beaufoy Publishing
11 Blenheim Court, 316 Woodstock Road, Oxford OX2 7NS, England
www.johnbeaufoy.com

10 9 8 7 6 5 4 3

ISBN 978-1-912081-37-0

PICTURE CREDITS

Leif Goodwin 112. Herman Lambert 123. Renée Lebeuf 75, 76. Tony Svensson 38. Shutterstock/Svitlyk 64. All other photographs by Paul Sterry and Andrew Merrick except for those on the following pages, which were supplied by Nature Photographers Ltd: S.C. Bisserot 155. Barry Hughes 20, 24, 47, 69, 72, 73, 145 (lower).
Page corner icons by Stephen Dew.

COVER PICTURES

All photographs by Paul Sterry, except as specified.
Front cover: Cep.
Back cover: *top* Morel; *middle* Jelly Ear; *bottom* Winter Chanterelle.© Shutterstock/Svitlyk.

DISCLAIMER

Great care has been taken to ensure the accuracy of the information contained in this work. However, neither the publisher nor the author can be held responsible for any consequences arising from use of the information
contained herein.

Edited, typeset and designed by
D & N Publishing, Baydon, Wiltshire, UK

Printed and bound in Malaysia by Times Offset (M) Sdn. Bhd.

CONTENTS

INTRODUCTION

Welcome to the fifth kingdom of living organisms – the kingdom of fungi. Fungi are living things that do not fit into the other four categories, i.e. the kingdoms of plants, animals, bacteria and protozoa. Like green plants they grow in the soil or on trees, but unlike them they do not contain chlorophyll and so cannot photosynthesise. They play an essential role in breaking down living and dead matter, absorbing their nutrients in the process, and as such are crucial to the nitrogen and nutrient cycles, along with insects and bacteria. In the words of the famous chef and mushroom enthusiast Antonio Carluccio, 'without fungi, human life would not be possible'.

The fungi in this book are all macrofungi – large fungi – of which between 3,000 and 5,000 species grow in northern Europe. No-one is quite sure how many there are, because better microscopy and the introduction of DNA sequencing to the study of taxonomy has meant that a fungus once considered to be a single species has now been discovered to be a group of several closely related species. This is the case with the Orange Birch Bolete (*Leccinum versipelle*). A Finnish researcher, Mauri Korhonen, has discovered that what appear to be mere variations in the colour of the cap are indications that these are a sub-species or even a separate species, although all are edible.

This book contains a representative selection of 150 of the most common and widespread species of fungus that grow throughout the United Kingdom and northern, central and eastern Europe, including those that are most highly prized for their flavour and those that are dangerously poisonous. Once you start hunting fungi, you will be amazed at their beauty and the variety of their colours and shapes.

The species are divided into three sections according to whether they are edible, not edible or poisonous. In each description, the calendar at the top of the page gives a rough indication of the months when the species can be found. The first item in each entry is the common name, followed by the scientific name. Below that, there is a description of the fungus and information about its edibility where relevant. Some fungi are edible and delicious, others are edible but not considered to be particularly tasty, and others still are inedible owing to their bitter or peppery taste, but are not poisonous. The accompanying Fact File provides details of the family to which the fungus belongs, synonyms for the names (many scientific names for fungi have changed several times over the years), the approximate size and other important facts.

EDIBLE MUSHROOMS 23

JAN FEB MAR APR MAY **JUN JUL AUG SEP OCT NOV** DEC

OCHRE BRITTLEGILL

Russula ochroleuca

The russulas or brittlegills are related to the milkcaps but do not exude milk when cut or bruised. They are very distinctive, generally with a brightly coloured cap and a straight, thick stem, and all parts of the fungi have a chalky, brittle consistency. The Ochre Brittlegill has an ochre-yellow cap that is domed at first, then flattening with a central depression. The flesh under the cap is yellow, shading to white, and the gills and sturdy stem are white.

Edible, but the flavour varies and is sometimes peppery. Pre-cook in butter and taste before adding to stews.

WHERE TO FIND

Grows under deciduous and coniferous trees at all altitudes.

FACT FILE

FAMILY Russulaceae CAP 5–10cm HEIGHT 4–9cm STATUS Widespread POSSIBLE CONFUSION Easily confused with the Yellow Swamp Brittlegill *R. claroflava*, whose cap is also yellow, but so are its gills; it only grows under birches and is often found in *Sphagnum* bogs

Fungi are difficult to photograph because their distinctive features – gills, stem and cap – are on different planes, and also because in nature those that grow on the ground may be almost completely buried in the earth or covered in a layer of humus, fallen leaves or pine needles. The photographs in this book aim to show different views of the fungi, but identification from a single image is not always reliable and so it is a good idea to carry more than one field guide with you on your forays.

GEOGRAPHICAL DISTRIBUTION

Because the spores of fungi are so light, they are carried into the upper atmosphere and thence the jetstream – as a result, many species can be found growing all over the world. This is true, for instance, of the Fly Agaric (p. 136), the familiar mushroom whose red cap is dotted with white spots, which is found as far north as Finland and as far south as New Zealand. Some fungi are limited to certain climatic zones, such as the early-fruiting St George's Mushroom (p. 37), found in April and as far south as Italy, where it fruits in March, and the delicious Caesar's Mushroom, a species confined to southern Europe that does not usually grow north of central France (although in particularly warm years it can be found as far north as Brittany).

All the fungi in this book are native to the United Kingdom and northern Europe. Not included are exotic fungi that have spread to Europe as accidental imports, such as the many new species found growing on imported tree bark and woodchip mulch. Devil's Fingers *Clathrus archeri*, a species native to Australia and New Zealand, reached France in 1914 on military equipment that was brought to Europe for the First World War; other exotic species have been introduced through the importation of plants from the tropics. Through such means, fungi are constantly spreading and new species are continuously being found outside their native habitat.

NOMENCLATURE

Until recently, many fungi had no common English names, mainly because people living in the English-speaking world did not pick wild mushrooms – unlike in Scandinavia and eastern Europe, where there is a mushroom-hunting tradition. The British Mycological Society (BMS) and the North American Mycological Association (NAMA) have now agreed on common English names for most of our native fungi. The better-known species did, however, have traditional names – sometimes several – and these continue to be used, often causing confusion. An example is the Field Blewit, an edible mushroom once sold in markets in Britain, which is also known as Blue Legs. Many of these quaint traditional names have now been accepted as the official name, such as Slippery Jack (p. 16) and Weeping Widow (p. 56), and there are equally evocative names for toxic species, such as Funeral Bell (p. 145) and Poisonpie (p. 146).

The scientific names for fungi are, unfortunately, in a state of flux. Mycology – the study of fungi – did not become a science until the late 18th to mid-19th centuries, and the early mycologists invented names for fungi using the Linnaean binomial system. This is the system whereby the genus name (e.g. *Lactarius*, *Russula*) comes first and is capitalised, and the second part of the name, the descriptive part, is the name of the species and is always lower case. The species name may describe the shape, colour or other features (e.g. *Phallus impudicus*, *Gomphidius roseus*, *Lepiota cristata*), or be derived from the name of a famous person, often a mycologist or naturalist (e.g. *Suillus grevillei*).

The early mycologists placed all gill fungi in the genus *Agaricus* and all pore fungi in the genus *Boletus*. Later, as the differences between fungi were recognised, new genera were created. The more recent advent of DNA sequencing has caused an extensive regrouping of species and the creation of yet more new genera, such that it is often hard to keep up with the new names. For instance, until recently the tropical stinkhorn-like fungi that have a reticulated veil extending down from the cap to the pseudo-stem were placed in the genus *Dictyophora*. Mycologists have since discovered that all the stinkhorns have a similar veil, even if in the European species (such as *Phallus impudicus*, p. 106) it is vestigial, so all stinkhorns are now placed together in the genus *Phallus*. Many people are not aware of this change, however, and continue to use the separate genus name *Dictyophora*.

ANATOMY OF A MUSHROOM

When you pick a mushroom, you actually only pick the fruiting body of the fungus. The fungus itself is a mass of thread-like structures known as the mycelium, which in turn consist of microscopic tubes called hyphae.

Some fungi are parasites, living off a host and eventually killing it, while others are saprophytes, living off dead material. Others still are a combination of the two, killing a tree and then living off it, an example being the Chicken of the Woods (p. 69). Many parasitic fungi infect trees through the growth of clumped hyphae called rhizomorphs, which are thick, root-like structures that are able to travel from tree to tree. Yet other fungi have a symbiotic relationship with trees, feeding nutrients to the tree via its roots that it would not be able to access otherwise, and in return gaining sugars from the tree, a process known as mycorrhizal association. Saplings transplanted from their native habitat may fail to thrive because the fungi with which they are associated are not brought along with them. Since these relationships have been discovered, such saplings are generally transported with their symbiotic fungi, making all the difference to their survival rates.

IDENTIFICATION

Gill fungi can be hard to identify. One way is to look at the colour of the spores. Since spores are microscopic, the best way to see their colour is to make a spore print. To do so, take a piece of white or blue paper, cut off the cap of the fungus at the top of stem, and place the cap, gills downwards, on the paper. Leave it in a dry, draught-free place overnight. The next day, carefully remove the cap and you will have a perfect spore print.

Fungi are also identifiable by their stem. Look to see if it has a ring, and check the shape of the base of the stem. Some fungi grow from a universal veil that envelops the entire fungus when young, like the shell of an egg. The remnants of this veil often remain at the base of the stem, as in the *Volvariella* genus, or leave frills on it or warts on the cap, as in the Fly Agaric (p. 136).

The shape of the gills and the way in which they are attached to the stem are also important identifiers. Gills may be adnate, adnexed, decurrent or free, or they may be sinuate or toothed in shape. They may be crowded or distant, regular or uneven.

Always make sure you have identified a fungus correctly before you attempt to eat it. Go through the above features in a checklist, and if you have any doubts at all then discard it. If you are a novice, eat only fungi that are easily identifiable.

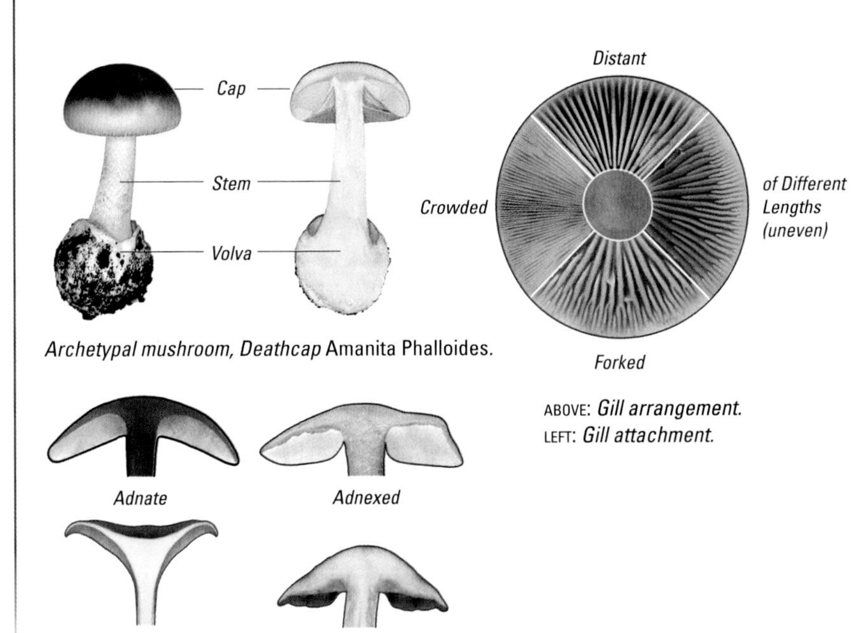

Archetypal mushroom, Deathcap Amanita Phalloides.

ABOVE: *Gill arrangement.*
LEFT: *Gill attachment.*

MUSHROOM HUNTING

Perhaps the most exciting aspect of mushroom hunting is that you never know what you are going to find. One season, you may find mushrooms growing in a particular spot, and then you never see them there again for the next 10 or even 20 years!

The seasonal information in this book is only a rough guide. In years in which there is little rain, fungi may not appear until later than their usual growing season; in other years, if the summer is wet, they will emerge earlier. For instance, in 2011, autumn in the south of England was exceptionally dry and it was not until November and December that some of the early-autumn mushrooms appeared. That same year, Ceps (p. 10) and Horns of Plenty (p. 63) were found in abundance in early autumn in central Sweden, where the summer rains had been average but there had been an exceptionally long warm spell.

Many fungi are hard to spot, which is why children are so valuable on a fungus hunt. Their eyes are sharper and nearer the ground, and they will find species that you might miss altogether. Their other advantage is that you can hoist them onto your shoulders and get them to cut down higher outcrops of tree-growing fungi!

Fungi have different lifespans: many tree-growing species are tough and continue to grow for several years, but some of the fragile mushrooms growing in grass may last only a single day. The best time for picking the latter is the early morning, especially on warm days, when they might shrivel in the sun.

Collared Earthstar Geastrum triplex *(p. 127).*

Fly Agaric Amanita muscaria *(p. 136).*

The only equipment you will need are a collecting basket made of wicker or willow, or even one of those very light ones made of strong paper in which cultivated mushrooms are marketed; some paper bags and a sharp knife. Special mushroom-hunting knives can be bought on the Internet, with a brush attachment for cleaning the fungi, but any small sharp knife and a small soft brush should be adequate. Do not, however, slice mushrooms off across the stem when you find them. Instead, dig them carefully out of the substrate with the base of the stem intact, or you may well leave behind an important identification feature, such as a volva or bulbous base.

Place the different species in separate paper bags, especially if you pick a fungus that is known to be poisonous, because its spores will also be poisonous and might contaminate your other finds. Never put fungi in a polythene or plastic bag, as their exhalations will condense inside the bag and rot the mushrooms. For tough tree-growing varieties, you may need a bigger knife (some American authorities recommend an axe!) to cut them down. If you are carrying a knife, remember to wrap it well when travelling.

It is a good idea to take a magnifying glass or jeweller's loupe to identify minute characteristics. Really sophisticated hunters also carry small bottles of potassium hydroxide and household ammonia, fitted with an eye dropper, to drop on the flesh or gills, as the colour reaction helps in identification.

Try to look for fungi in as wide a range of locations as possible – fields and woods, inland and by the sea, among deciduous and coniferous trees, at sea-level and in the mountains. You will

Common Earthball Scleroderma citrinum *(p. 156).*

find them growing everywhere, including, if you are unlucky, on the structural timbers of your house or on a damp carpet! I once visited a friend's house to go on a foray with him, and we found our first tiny mushroom growing on his front doorstep!

You do not have to go striding the hills, dales or primeval forests to find fungi. If you live in town, you will find many varieties growing in gardens, your local park, and especially on common land, heaths and in the rough on golf courses, where natural growth has not been killed off by overzealous lawnmowing, fertilising, weeding or pruning. Fungi absorb more nutrients from their surroundings than any other organism, so never pick specimens on polluted ground in locations where they are likely to be contaminated by heavy metals or other poisons, such as beside major roads.

KEEPING AND STORING MUSHROOMS

Fungi are generally fragile and do not keep well, except when dried (*see* below). Back at home with your finds, slice off any rotten, damaged or dirty parts, wipe the fungi with a cloth and then refrigerate them as soon as possible. Do not keep them for more than three days – less for fungi that deliquesce, such as the inkcaps. If you are going to dry them, start doing so as soon as possible.

Fungi can be preserved by pickling or canning, but in the process they will lose most of their flavour. If you do not want to eat them immediately, cook them in a little water or fry them in butter or oil, then store them in the refrigerator in a glass or ceramic bowl or jar, covered with clingfilm. This way, they will keep for at least a week. Raw mushrooms cannot be frozen, as the cell walls break down in most species, but like many fragile vegetables they can be frozen after cooking.

COOKING WITH MUSHROOMS

Wild mushrooms – even Field Mushrooms (p. 52) – are juicier and tastier than shop-bought mushrooms. They can be used to enhance the flavour of bland or unexciting foods, but their delicate, subtle taste should never be masked or drowned by strong spices and flavourings.

All fungi should be cooked within three days of picking. Do not wash mushrooms, but instead scrape off any debris with a sharp knife and then wipe them with a damp cloth or dampened kitchen paper. If you are new to wild mushrooms, do not mix several species in one dish but keep them separate. Some people have allergic reactions to fungi, just as they do to strawberries or shellfish, but these are invariably limited to individual species. By cooking with only one species, any such reactions can easily be isolated and the mushroom in question then avoided in future. There are even fungi that will give one person an upset stomach and leave another totally unaffected.

Many species of fungi can be dried for preservation, including all the boletes. Discard the spongy pores and tough stem, slice the flesh thinly, then thread the pieces on a nylon thread and hang up in a warm, dry place, such as over a kitchen stove. They can also be dried in a drying oven or, if laid out in well-spaced rows on a metal baking sheet, left overnight in a gas oven with only the pilot light on or in an electric oven on the lowest setting. Other mushrooms that dry well are the Fairy Ring Champignon (p. 43), the Chanterelle (p. 62) and related species, the morels (of which there are several closely related species; pp. 82–3), the hedgehog mushrooms (p. 80) and the puffballs (but only when they are young, before the spore mass has changed colour from white; pp. 65–7).

To reconstitute dried fungi, soak them in hot water (about 125ml of water to 50g of dried fungi) for 15 minutes. The soaking water can be used for cooking, but strain it first as it may contain sand and debris.

Wild mushrooms are a traditional accompaniment to game. Chanterelles, for example (p. 62), are eaten with venison all over Europe, and morels are a wonderful addition to bread and herb stuffing for gamebirds bred for the table, such as quail.

A favourite way to cook fleshy gill mushrooms is to slice them and poach them for about 10 minutes in a saucepan with a tight-fitting lid in a little chicken or vegetable stock (about 50ml to 60g of sliced fresh mushrooms), the juice of half a lemon, and some salt and pepper. The same recipe can be used for a microwave oven, in which case the mushrooms will not need more than three minutes' cooking time.

Mushrooms are also delicious fried in butter or oil and added to an omelette or other egg dish. Always cook the mushrooms separately before adding them to the eggs, to ensure that they are cooked thoroughly. They also make a tasty topping for open sandwiches and bruschetta, and of course they make delicious soup.

GLOSSARY

I have tried to keep the use of technical terms to a minimum in the species descriptions in this book, but a few have crept in because there are no simple alternatives. Here is a very short list of those I have been unable to avoid, as well as a few more you are likely to encounter in other books.

Adnate Gills or tubes attached to the stem at one end along their entire width.

Adnexed Gills or tubes narrowly attached to the stem by part of their width.

Ascomycete Fungus belonging to the phylum Ascomycota, in which the spores are contained in small sacs called asci.

Ascus (pl. asci) The small sacs, usually holding eight spores, in which the spores of an ascomycete are contained.

Basidiomycete Fungus belonging to the phylum Basidomycota, in which the spores are attached to club-shaped structures known as basidia.

Basidium (pl. basidia) The club-shaped structures on which the spores of basidomycetes are held. Most of the larger fungi are basidiomycetes.

Club fungi Fungi that have no cap or gills, but which consist of a club-shaped or branched structure rising from a single stem.

Cortina The thin, fragile veil that covers the gills of certain genera of fungi, such as *Cortinarius*.

Decurrent Gills, veins, spines or other structures under the cap of mushroom that run down the stem.

Deliquescence The tendency of certain fungi, especially the inkcaps, to liquefy or melt as they age.

Depressed Having a depression or hollow somewhere on the cap, often in the centre.

Eccentric Where the cap, gills or pores are off-centre.

Fibril A tiny fibrous scale or hair.

Imbricated Where caps are piled one on top of the other, as in the Oyster Mushroom (p. 59).

Macrofungus A fungus whose major structures (cap, gills, stem) are visible to the naked eye.

Microfungus A fungus whose major structures are invisible to the naked eye, such as a mould or mildew. Most fungi are microfungi.

Mycelium The network of filaments, usually too small to be seen by the naked eye, that are the true body of the fungus, and from which the visible part, the sporophore or fruiting body, grows.

Ozonium A thick, shaggy carpet of mycelium produced by a few macrofungi, especially the Firerug Inkcap (p. 102).

Persistent A part of a fungus that lasts from first fruiting to maturity.

Reticulation The appearance of 'netting' over the surface.

Resupinate Lying flat, in the shape of a crust or thin layer.

Sporophore Another name for the fruiting body or large visible part of a macrofungus, which is, in fact, the fruit of the mycelium.

Umbo A small protuberance or mound in the centre of the cap of some species.

Universal veil A membrane that totally covers the young specimens of certain fungi, such as the Fly Agaric (p. 136).

Volva Cup-shaped remnant of the universal veil, covering the base of the stem in certain species, such as the amanitas.

Zoned A term describing the concentric circles that decorate the cap of certain species, such as the milkcaps and some of the polypores.

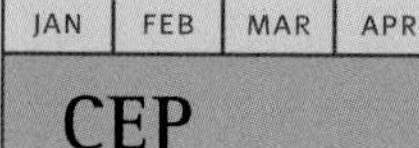

JAN FEB MAR APR MAY JUN **JUL AUG SEP OCT** NOV DEC

CEP

Boletus edulis

WHERE TO FIND

In grass and under ferns in oak woods; occasioanally under pines.

As in all boletes, the underside of the cap consists of tubes ending in pores, not gills. The cap can be various shades of brown. The pores are white, ageing to yellow or brown. The most typical feature is the bulbous off-white stem, which is very thick, sometimes wider than the cap, and covered in white reticulation. The pale yellow to whitish flesh does not change colour when cut.

Edible and delicious, although it is often attacked by insects and other animals, and the stem is usually too tough to eat in older specimens. One of the few wild fungi that is safe to eat when raw if in good condition and thoroughly cleaned first. Ceps have a smoky, spicy flavour and can be fried, stewed or steamed. They make a wonderful sauce if cooked with crème fraîche, chopped walnuts and a chopped garlic clove; this can be poured over pasta or served with veal or chicken. Ceps also make an excellent soup if simmered with chicken, veal or vegetable stock. They can be dried if the tubes are cut away.

FACT FILE

FAMILY **Boletaceae** SYNONYMS **Penny Bun, Porcini** CAP **6–25cm** HEIGHT **6–25cm** STATUS **Widespread** POSSIBLE CONFUSION **Similar to other brown-capped boletes, but unlikely to be confused with any poisonous or inedible species**

JAN FEB MAR APR MAY JUN **JUL AUG SEP OCT** NOV DEC

SCARLETINA BOLETE

Boletus luridiformis

The cap is olive-brown. The pores on the cap underside are pale yellow, turning reddish brown with age as the brown spores ripen. The flesh is pale yellow turning deep blue when cut. The stem is yellow but so densely covered in red spots that it appears to be red.

Edible, but never eat it raw or consume it with alcohol. Prepare and cook it in the same way as Cep (p. 10). Can be dried if the tubes are cut away.

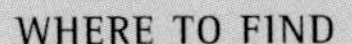

WHERE TO FIND

In deciduous, coniferous and mixed woods favouring acid soils.

FACT FILE

FAMILY Boletaceae SYNONYM *B. erythropus* CAP 6–20cm HEIGHT 6–20cm STATUS Widespread POSSIBLE CONFUSION May be mistaken for Lurid Bolete *B. luridus*, another edible red-stemmed bolete, which grows under oak, Beech *Fagus sylvatica* or lime and prefers limestone soils; Ruby Bolete *B. rubellus*, which has a red cap and is not edible; and the handsome Satan's Bolete *B. satanus*, with a red stem and pores and an off-white cap. The last species is rare and protected, and is one of the few poisonous boletes

JAN	FEB	MAR	APR	MAY	JUN	**JUL**	**AUG**	**SEP**	**OCT**	NOV	DEC

RED CRACKING BOLETE

Boletus cisalpinus

WHERE TO FIND

In deciduous woods, especially oak. Solitary or in small groups.

The cap is dark brown but soon cracks to reveal a red surface just beneath. The flesh is pale yellow and the pores on the cap underside are bright yellow, turning brown with age as the brown spores ripen. The stem is yellow at the top and streaked with red at the base. The flesh turns blue when cut.

Edible, but do not eat raw or consume with alcohol. Prepare and cook it in the same way as Cep (p. 10), but note that the flesh is softer. The flesh can be dried if the tubes are cut away.

Cracked cap revealing flesh underneath

PORES ON UNDERSIDE OF CAP.

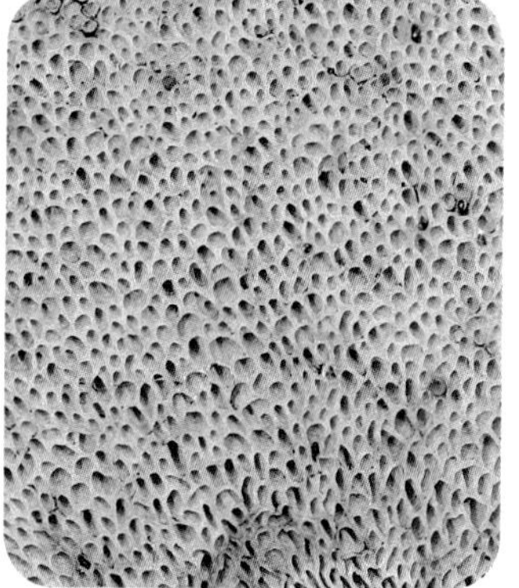

FACT FILE

FAMILY **Boletaceae** SYNONYM *Xerocomus cisalpinus* CAP **4–11cm** HEIGHT **5–13cm**
STATUS **Widespread** POSSIBLE CONFUSION *B. cisalpinus* has only recently been separated from *B. chrysenteron* and is easily confused with it. When cut *B. cisalpinus* turns blue, especially in the stem base and is most often found under oaks. *B. chrysenteron* does not turn blue when cut and is usually found with Beech and conifers. The surface of White-cracking Bolete *B. porosporus* also cracks but reveals white flesh beneath. All are edible

JAN FEB MAR APR MAY JUN **JUL AUG SEP OCT** NOV DEC

MATT BOLETE

Boletus pruinatus

The cap is dark brown and in dry weather is covered in a velvety whitish down, hence the species name. The pores on the underside of the cap are bright yellow, turning green with age. The flesh is pale yellow. The stem is yellow at the top and streaked with red at the base. The flesh turns blue when damaged or cut.

Edible, but do not eat raw or consume with alcohol. Prepare and cook it in the same way as Cep (p. 10). The flesh can be dried if the tubes are cut away.

WHERE TO FIND

Under broadleaf trees, especially oaks and Beech *Fagus sylvatica.*

FACT FILE

FAMILY **Boletaceae** SYNONYM *Xerocomus pruinatus* CAP **4–11cm** HEIGHT **5–13cm** STATUS **Widespread** POSSIBLE CONFUSION **Suede Bolete (p. 14) has a similar felty brown cap and a yellow stem. It hardly changes colour when cut and prefers acid soils**

JAN FEB MAR APR MAY JUN **JUL AUG SEP OCT** NOV DEC

SUEDE BOLETE

Boletus subtomentosus

WHERE TO FIND

Under deciduous and coniferous trees. Look for it alongside the Red Cracking Bolete (p. 12), with which it often grows.

The cap is dark brown, hemispherical at first, then flattening. In dry weather it feels velvety, hence the species' common name, and in occasional specimens it cracks. The pores on the underside of the cap are bright yellow, turning green with age as the brown spores ripen. The stem is yellowish and sometimes streaked with red. The flesh usually does not change colour when cut but does occasionally turn blue, normally only weakly but sometimes strongly.

Edible, but do not eat raw or consume with alcohol. Prepare and cook it in the same way as Cep (p. 10). The flesh can be dried if the tubes are cut away.

FACT FILE

FAMILY Boletaceae SYNONYM *Xerocomus subtomentosus* CAP 4–11cm HEIGHT 5–13cm STATUS Widespread POSSIBLE CONFUSION In atypical specimens in which the cap cracks, it could be confused with Red Cracking Bolete (p. 12) and Matt Bolete (p. 13)

JAN	FEB	MAR	APR	MAY	JUN	**JUL**	**AUG**	**SEP**	**OCT**	NOV	DEC

ORANGE OAK BOLETE

Leccinum aurantiacum

Leccinum boletes have a distinctive white stem covered in coarse tufts. The cap of this bolete is a distinctive orange colour and feels velvety in dry weather. The flesh is thick and whitish, darkening to pinkish grey when cut. The pores on the underside of the cap are small and white, turning greyish brown with age. The stem is white and covered in dark orange tufts. The smell and taste are pleasant.

Edible when young. Prepare and cook it in the same way as Cep (p. 10). The flesh can be dried if the pores are cut away.

WHERE TO FIND

In mixed woods, mainly under oaks, Aspen *Populus tremula* and other poplars. Prefers a damp clay soil.

FACT FILE

FAMILY Boletaceae SYNONYMS *L. quercinum*, *Boletus aurantiacus* CAP 10–20cm HEIGHT 6–15cm STATUS Widespread POSSIBLE CONFUSION Orange Birch Bolete *L. versipelle* is similar, but its stem scales are black and is confined to birches. It is also edible

JAN | FEB | MAR | APR | **MAY** | **JUN** | **JUL** | **AUG** | **SEP** | OCT | NOV | DEC

SLIPPERY JACK

Suillus luteus

WHERE TO FIND

Grows in groups under pine trees, especially on high ground. Fruits earlier than most autumn fungi.

This bolete is distinguished by its slimy chestnut-brown cap and large, thick ring on the stem. The ring is white at first, darkening with age, and is the remains of a veil that covers the pores in young specimens; sometimes fragments of the veil cling to the edge of the cap. The whitish flesh is thick. The pores and tubes are yellow, darkening to ochre with age. The cylindrical stem is yellow with brown dots above the ring, and white below it. The flesh does not change colour when cut.

Edible, but the slime should first be scraped from the cap. Prepare and cook it in the same way as Cep (p. 10). The flesh can be dried if the pores are cut away.

FACT FILE

FAMILY Suillaceae CAP 5–12cm HEIGHT 7–13cm STATUS Widespread POSSIBLE CONFUSION Almost all species in the genus *Suillus* have slimy caps; none is poisonous

VELVET BOLETE

Suillus variegatus

Associated with conifers.

The downy cap, which starts off dry becomes greasy with age, is dark brown to olive and distinctively spotted with small, darker scales. The pores on the underside of the cap are ochre, turning brown with age as the brown spores ripen. The stem is yellow at the top and ochre at the base. The flesh is pale yellow, slowly turning pale blue when cut, especially in the stem. There is no ring.

Prepare and cook it in the same way as Cep (p. 10). The flesh can be dried if the pores are cut away.

LEFT: *OCHRE PORES ON UNDERSIDE OF CAP.*

FACT FILE

FAMILY **Suillaceae** SYNONYM **Variegated Bolete** CAP **6–13cm** HEIGHT **5–8cm** STATUS **Widespread but uncommon** POSSIBLE CONFUSION **In atypical specimens in which the cap cracks, it could be confused with *Boletus cisalpinus***

JAN FEB MAR APR MAY JUN **JUL AUG SEP OCT** NOV DEC

LARCH BOLETE

Suillus grevillei

WHERE TO FIND

Grows exclusively under larches.

This fungus is entirely yellow, though ranges from daffodil-yellow to pale brownish yellow. In immature specimens the cap is pale brown. The fluffy white veil covers the pores in young specimens and tears into a ring as the fungus grows. The flesh is pale yellow under the cap and bright yellow on the stem above the ring. Below the ring, the stem darkens and is covered with red veins or spots, which vary from prominent to barely visible. The yellow pores turn brown with age.

Prepare and cook it in the same way as Cep (p. 10). The flesh can be dried if the pores are cut away.

ABOVE: *YELLOW PORES.*

FACT FILE

FAMILY Suillaceae SYNONYMS Elegant Bolete, *Boletus elegans*, *B. grevillei* CAP 5–10cm HEIGHT 6–10cm STATUS Widespread POSSIBLE CONFUSION Other boletes with slimy caps and a ring on the stem could be mistaken for Larch Bolete, especially young specimens; all such boletes are edible

PEPPERY MILKCAP

Lactarius piperatus

Milkcaps are fungi with gills like the Cultivated Mushroom *Agaricus bisporus*, but all exude a milky substance when the cap and gills are cut or bruised. The cap, gills, flesh, stem and milk of the Peppery Milkcap are all white. The cap is smooth and shiny in wet weather, and is funnel-shaped, the edge remaining inrolled for a long time. The gills are usually decurrent and crowded. The milk is abundant, and the whole fungus, including the milk, has a strongly peppery taste.

Owing to its peppery taste, the species is not a popular edible fungus except in E Europe, where its flavour is much appreciated in stews with other fungi. Stew it in a little milk, so that the flavour is less fiery, then mix it with vegetables such as Brussels sprouts and grated cabbage. Its pepperiness also makes it a good curry ingredient.

WHERE TO FIND

Found on the ground in damp places in deciduous woods. Look for it under the tips of tree branches, where the leaves drip most of their moisture.

FACT FILE

FAMILY Russulaceae CAP 10–16cm HEIGHT 6–8cm STATUS Widespread POSSIBLE CONFUSION May be confused with other all-white species, but the milk is the key identifying factor

JAN	FEB	MAR	APR	MAY	JUN	**JUL**	**AUG**	**SEP**	**OCT**	NOV	DEC

FALSE SAFFRON MILKCAP

Lactarius deterrimus

WHERE TO FIND

Grows only under spruces.

Has an orange cap stained with green, and bright orange gills and stem. The green staining can also be seen on the gills as the fungus ages. The smooth cap has a central depression and is inrolled when young, and the gills run down the thick stem. The flesh is orange except in the middle of the stem where it is whitish. The milk is bright orange, but turns red after exposure to air for between 10 and 30 minutes, which is the main feature distinguishing this species from the Saffron Milkcap (p. 21).

Edible, although some people find it bitter. Not to be eaten raw, and best cooked by frying or adding to egg dishes and meat stews. It is believed to have medicinal properties and is an antioxidant.

FACT FILE

FAMILY Russulaceae CAP 5–10cm HEIGHT 2.5–7cm STATUS Widespread

POSSIBLE CONFUSION Saffron Milkcap (p. 21) and, possibly, Woolly Milkcap (p. 22)

SAFFRON MILKCAP

Lactarius deliciosus

The cap is inrolled, becoming wavy and depressed in the centre; it is pale orange with darker orange concentric rings, and green patches appear with age. The pinkish-orange gills are tightly packed, spotting green with age like the cap. The flesh is pale yellow to orange. There is dark pitting on the stem. The smell is fruity and slightly spicy. The orange milk is unchanging or reddens only after 30 minutes exposure to air.

Edible and delicious. Sauté gently in butter and serve with mashed potatoes.

WHERE TO FIND

Grows exclusively under pines. Prefers sandy soils.

FACT FILE

FAMILY Russulaceae CAP 5–12cm HEIGHT 4–8cm STATUS Widespread POSSIBLE CONFUSION Easily confused with the False Saffron Milkcap (p. 20), whose milk turns red more quickly on exposure to air, and which has a different habitat. Also possibly confused with the Woolly Milkcap (p. 22)

JAN | FEB | MAR | APR | MAY | JUN | **JUL** | **AUG** | **SEP** | **OCT** | NOV | DEC

WOOLLY MILKCAP

Lactarius torminosus

WHERE TO FIND

Only grows under birches.

The cap is a uniform pink with concentric whitish rings (concentric rings on the cap are another feature typical of milkcaps). The edge of the cap is inrolled and covered in shaggy, beard-like hairs in young specimens, becoming smoother in old specimens. The milk or latex is white and does not change colour as in some other milkcaps. The crowded gills are cream or pink, as is the flesh. The thick stem is the same colour as the gills and is occasionally slightly pitted or with darker spots.

Edible but very peppery.

FACT FILE

FAMILY Russulaceae CAP 4–9cm HEIGHT 4–8cm STATUS Widespread POSSIBLE CONFUSION Bearded Milkcap *L. pubescens* is similar but less hairy, smaller and paler. False Saffron Milkcap (p. 20) and Saffron Milkcap (p. 21) are also similar in outward appearance but their milk is a different colour

JAN	FEB	MAR	APR	MAY	**JUN**	**JUL**	**AUG**	**SEP**	**OCT**	**NOV**	DEC

OCHRE BRITTLEGILL

Russula ochroleuca

WHERE TO FIND

Grows under deciduous and coniferous trees at all altitudes.

The russulas or brittlegills are related to the milkcaps but do not exude milk when cut or bruised. They are very distinctive, generally with a brightly coloured cap and a straight, thick stem, and all parts of the fungi have a chalky, brittle consistency. The Ochre Brittlegill has an ochre-yellow cap that is domed at first, then flattening with a central depression. The flesh under the cap is yellow, shading to white, and the gills and sturdy stem are white.

Edible, but the flavour varies and is sometimes peppery. Pre-cook in butter and taste before adding to stews.

FACT FILE

FAMILY Russulaceae CAP 5–10cm HEIGHT 4–9cm STATUS Widespread POSSIBLE CONFUSION Easily confused with the Yellow Swamp Brittlegill *R. claroflava*, whose cap is also yellow, but so are its gills; it only grows under birches and is often found in *Sphagnum* bogs

JAN	FEB	MAR	APR	MAY	**JUN**	**JUL**	**AUG**	**SEP**	OCT	NOV	DEC

TALL BRITTLEGILL

Russula paludosa

WHERE TO FIND

Grows under conifers, preferring damp places. In Britain it is virtually confined to Scotland where it is common.

The cap is pink to reddish and domed at first, becoming flat with a central depression. The whitish to yellow gills are attached to the tall white stem and are widely spaced. The spores are ochre. The flesh under the cap is yellow, shading to white.

Edible; sold in Finnish markets.

FACT FILE

FAMILY Russulaceae CAP 4–14cm HEIGHT 5–15cm STATUS Widespread but uncommon
POSSIBLE CONFUSION Easily confused with other red-capped brittlegills such as The Sickener *R. emetica*, which as its name implies is definitely not edible

JAN | FEB | MAR | APR | MAY | **JUN** | **JUL** | **AUG** | **SEP** | **OCT** | **NOV** | DEC

CHARCOAL BURNER

Russula cyanoxantha

The colour of the cap varies considerably in this species, often containing patches of different hues – mostly green, violet and black – but it can be brownish or greenish: colours similar to the burning of a charcoal flame, which gives the mushroom its common name.
The cap is domed when young, later flattening and becoming slightly depressed in the centre. The waxy white gills are flexible, narrow and crowded. The edge of the cap is sometimes slightly wrinkled. The flesh of the cap and stem is white, but pinkish under the cuticle.

Edible and delicious, sold in German markets. Trim away the tough stem and sauté the caps in butter and lemon juice.

WHERE TO FIND

Found under a wide range of both deciduous and coniferous trees, often in large numbers.

FACT FILE

FAMILY Russulaceae CAP 5–12cm HEIGHT 4–8cm STATUS Widespread POSSIBLE CONFUSION May be confused with *R. grisea*, which has a grey-brown cap, grows mostly under Beech and is also edible; or with the Ugly Milkcap *Lactarius turpis*, which also has a black cap but exudes milk and is not edible

JAN FEB MAR APR **MAY JUN JUL AUG SEP** OCT NOV DEC

PARASOL

Macrolepiota procera

WHERE TO FIND

Grows in small groups in grassland, often at the edge of woods in siliceous soil. Look for it in early autumn, when it fruits.

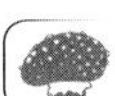

This striking mushroom is one of the largest European fungi. All fungi in the genera *Macrolepiota*, *Chlorophyllum* and *Lepiota* have tall, narrow stems in which a veil covers the gills in the early stages, this breaking to form a thick double ring in some species. The gills and flesh are off-white. The Parasol's cap is of various shades of white, covered in large, dark brown scales with a large central scale at the often pointed top, hence the species' popular name. The tall stem is narrow and also covered in brown scales. The young Parasol has a distinctive appearance, resembling a drumstick.

Edible and delicious. The Parasol can be poached, as it has a similar flavour to smoked fish. Discard the tough stem and place the cap in a frying pan to which a little water and the juice of half a lemon has been added. Cover and simmer on low heat for 7 minutes.

FACT FILE

FAMILY Agaricaceae SYNONYM *Lepiota procera* CAP 25–40cm HEIGHT 12–30cm
STATUS Widespread POSSIBLE CONFUSION All of the smaller species of *Lepiota*, of which the best known is the Stinking Dapperling (p. 135), can be confused with the Parasol and are poisonous. Related species that have green gills also look similar and are poisonous, but they do not grow in N Europe. The edible Shaggy Parasol (p. 27) may also be mistaken for this species

SHAGGY PARASOL

Chlorophyllum rhacodes

WHERE TO FIND

Mainly grows under deciduous trees. Best looked for in early autumn.

The Shaggy Parasol is smaller than the Parasol (p. 26), but is still one of the larger cap mushrooms. The stem lacks scales and is white with a distinctly bulbous base. It has a veil that covers the gills in the early stages, this breaking into a thick double ring in mature specimens. The shaggy cap is covered in large, dark brown scales on a whitish background. The flesh reddens when cut or bruised. The young Shaggy Parasol also has the drumstick appearance of the Parasol.

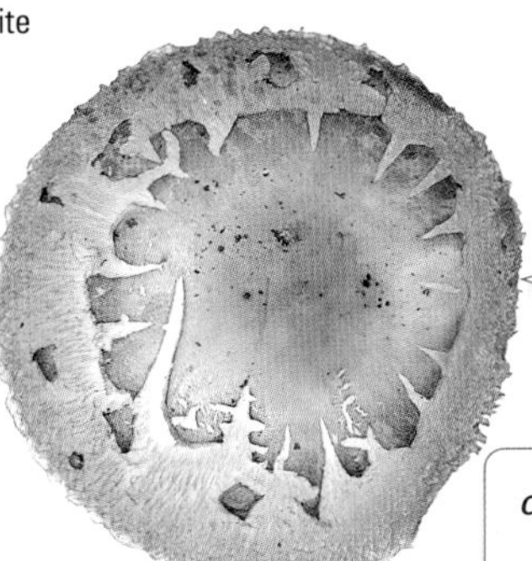

Centre of cap covered in large brown scale

Edible and delicious, but discard the stem. Cook in the same way as the Parasol.

Flesh reddens when cut or bruised

'Drumstick' shape of young specimens

FACT FILE

FAMILY Agaricaceae
SYNONYM *Macrolepiota rhacodes*, *Lepiota rhacodes* CAP 5–15cm
HEIGHT 12–20cm STATUS Widespread POSSIBLE CONFUSION Similar to the edible Parasol (p. 26). *C. olivieri* is similar but mostly found in coniferous woods and is also edible. The very similar *Macrolepiota venenata* has been responsible for stomach upsets, but prefers warm sites such as glasshouses and fields in the Mediterranean region, and the flesh does not redden

JAN	FEB	MAR	APR	MAY	JUN	**JUL**	**AUG**	**SEP**	**OCT**	NOV	DEC

THE BLUSHER

Amanita rubescens

WHERE TO FIND

Under trees in mixed woodlands.

The Blusher has a cap that varies in colour from pinkish brown to dark brown and is densely covered in whitish to reddish brown veil fragments; these disappear as the fungus matures. The cap is convex at first, flattening with age. The flesh, stem and gills are all white but the flesh turns pink to red when cut or damaged, hence the species' name. This distinctive feature distinguishes The Blusher from its poisonous lookalikes. It has a wide, frilly white ring and a bulbous stem covered in the remains of the volva.

Edible but must not be eaten raw. There are varying opinions as to how tasty it is. Discard the stem and fry the soft flesh in butter.

FACT FILE

FAMILY Amanitaceae CAP 8–15cm HEIGHT 8–12cm STATUS Widespread POSSIBLE CONFUSION Looks similar to the poisonous Panther Cap *A. pantherina*, which has a smooth brown cap and fewer pure white wart-like fragments, and the Grey Spotted Amanita *A. excelsa* var. *spissa*, whose cap fragments are greyer and which is not edible. However, the flesh does not change colour in either of these mushrooms

GRISETTE

Amanita vaginata

Despite looking fairly different from most amanitas – in particular lacking a ring – this species and Tawny Grisette *A. fulva* belong to the same genus. The Grisette has a grey cap that is deeply striated at the edge and extends until it is almost flat at maturity with a small central umbo. The tall stem narrows at the top and ends in a bulb at the base, sheathed in a volva that persists throughout the life of the fungus. The white stem may be covered in tiny fibrils. There is an all-white variety, var. *alba*.

Edible but must not be eaten raw. The firm flesh can be fried and added to omelettes.

WHERE TO FIND

Associated with Beech *Fagus sylvatica* and with spruces at high altitude.

FACT FILE

FAMILY Amanitaceae
SYNONYM *Amanitopsis vaginata*
CAP 5–10cm HEIGHT 8–12cm
STATUS Widespread
POSSIBLE CONFUSION The Tawny Grisette is very similar but its cap is golden brown and the white stem is sometimes tinged with brown as it ages. It has a similar habitat to the Grisette and is also edible

JAN | FEB | MAR | APR | MAY | JUN | **JUL** | **AUG** | **SEP** | **OCT** | **NOV** | DEC

MEADOW WAXCAP

Hygrocybe pratensis

WHERE TO FIND

Grows in clumps on well-drained grassland and beside paths.

The cap is apricot- to salmon-coloured and is bell-shaped at first, flattening to hemispherical in older specimens. The cap margin is uneven. The flesh is pale orange under the cap, which is thinner at the margin and sometimes depressed in the centre, while retaining a wide umbo. The stem is sturdy, thinning towards the base and often curved, and is similar in colour to the cap but paler. It is smooth and easily broken. The spores are white.

Edible, but no waxcap is really worth eating owing to the thin flesh.

FACT FILE

FAMILY Hygrophoraceae SYNONYMS *Hygrophorus pratensis, Camarophyllus pratensis, Cuphophyllus pratensis* CAP 3–8cm HEIGHT 4–7cm STATUS Widespread POSSIBLE CONFUSION Some forms of the Parrot Waxcap (p. 90) are similar in colour but have a slimy cap

GIRDLED KNIGHT

Tricholoma cingulatum

WHERE TO FIND

Found in association with willows, sometimes in sand-dunes.

The tricholomas are large, fleshy fungi. The stem is usually tall and thick, and may or may not have a ring. The common English name of members of the genus often includes the word 'knight' owing to the fact that the cap is saddle-shaped when the fungi are mature. In the Girdled Knight, the felty grey-brown cap is convex when expanded but retains a darker central umbo. In mature specimens the very edge of the cap is upturned and white. The gills are off-white and fairly crowded. The flesh is white and said to taste and smell of meal. There is a fluffy ring on the stem, which is tall, white and smooth.

Slice thickly and fry in oil or butter. Serve as an accompaniment to meat or fish.

FACT FILE

FAMILY Tricholomataceae SYNONYM *T. ramentaceum* CAP 3.5–6cm HEIGHT 7–12cm STATUS Widespread but occasional POSSIBLE CONFUSION May easily be mistaken for other grey-capped tricholomas such as the Grey Knight *T. terreum*, *T. sciodes* and the Mousy Tricholoma *T. myomyces* but none of these has a fluffy ring

JAN	FEB	MAR	APR	MAY	JUN	**JUL**	**AUG**	**SEP**	**OCT**	NOV	DEC

ANISEED FUNNEL

Clitocybe odora

WHERE TO FIND

Mainly found under Beech *Fagus sylvatica*, birches and spruces.

The cap of this small but distinctive funnelcap is an attractive grey-blue colour that turns greyish green or greyish brown in older specimens. The gills run a little way down the stem and are off-white, turning greyish green when older. The flesh is soft and white. The cylindrical stem is sturdy and ends in fluffy white mycelium at the base – another distinctive feature.

Edible, with a strong aniseed smell and flavour. It should be cooked and eaten by itself so that its flavour does not taint other foods.

FACT FILE

FAMILY **Tricholomataceae** CAP **4–8cm** HEIGHT **4–6cm** STATUS **Widespread but uncommon**

RUSSET TOUGHSHANK

Gymnopus dryophilus

Grows on humus and leaf litter.

The tawny or reddish-brown cap is slightly greasy in wet weather and has an incurving margin when young. The gills are white to pale cream, darkening with age. The thin flesh is white, but yellow just under the cap. The stem may be fibrous or smooth, the same colour or paler than the cap. The spores are white.

Discard the stem and fry in butter with a little lemon juice.

FACT FILE

FAMILY Tricholomataceae
SYNONYM *Collybia dryophila*
CAP 1–7.5cm HEIGHT 6–9cm
STATUS Widespread and common
NOTE Sometimes attacked by a parasitic fungus *Syzygospora mycetophila*, which produces pale growths on its stem and makes it inedible

JAN FEB MAR APR MAY JUN **JUL AUG SEP OCT NOV** DEC

SPINDLE TOUGHSHANK

Gymnopus fusipes

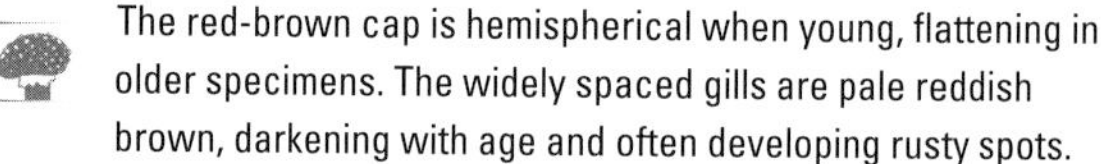

WHERE TO FIND

Grows in large clumps, joined together at the base, on roots of living trees, especially oak.

The red-brown cap is hemispherical when young, flattening in older specimens. The widely spaced gills are pale reddish brown, darkening with age and often developing rusty spots. The thick flesh is white, but yellow just under the cap. The long, light brown root-like stem is smooth and paler than the cap; it is narrow at the top, swollen in the middle and tapers at the base, where it is joined to other specimens – a typical feature. The spores are white.

Cook as for Russet Toughshank (p. 33).

FACT FILE

FAMILY Tricholomataceae
SYNONYMS *Collybia fusipes*, Spindleshank
CAP 1–7.5cm HEIGHT 6–9cm
STATUS Widespread and common

Spindle-shaped stem, sometimes grooved

Specimens grow in clumps, often fused together at the stem

TAWNY FUNNEL

Lepista flaccida

The cap colour is variable and ranges from pale brown to orange-brown, with older specimens often tawny brown. It is convex at first, with a central depression, becoming funnel-shaped as it ages. The crowded gills, which run down the stem, are creamy, as is the flesh, which is thick under the cap. The spores are white. The stem is sometimes eccentric.

Edible but not particularly good.

WHERE TO FIND

Grows in groups, the caps overlapping, on leaf litter under deciduous and coniferous trees.

FACT FILE

FAMILY Tricholomataceae SYNONYM *L. inversa* CAP 4–10cm
HEIGHT 5–10cm STATUS Widespread and common

JAN	FEB	MAR	APR	MAY	JUN	JUL	AUG	SEP	**OCT**	**NOV**	**DEC**

WOOD BLEWIT

Lepista nuda

WHERE TO FIND

Grows in coniferous and deciduous woods. This is a late species, persisting into winter, so may stand out at this time of year.

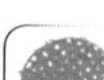

The fleshy cap is dove-grey, brown in the centre and shot with violet. The gills are crowded and are bright violet, fading brownish with age. The flesh is thick and lilac-coloured. The sturdy stem is pale violet and covered in white fibrils. The spores are pale pink.

Edible and delicious. Use it in any recipe for Cultivated Mushrooms but discard the stems. Makes an excellent duxelles – chop the fungi finely and cook almost to a paste in butter with onions.

FACT FILE

FAMILY Tricholomataceae SYNONYMS *Tricholoma nudum*, Blue Foot, Blue Stalk CAP 5–15cm HEIGHT 6–12cm STATUS Widespread and common in some years POSSIBLE CONFUSION The Lesser Blue Foot *L. sordida*, also edible, looks similar but is half the size; it grows in woods and grassland. The Field Blewit *L. saeva* is also similar, and mostly grey with white gills and a violet-tinted stem; it grows in grassland and is edible. Wood Blewit may also be confused with the poisonous Lilac Bonnet (p. 141)

ST GEORGE'S MUSHROOM

Calocybe gambosa

This species, so called because it is usually found around St George's Day (23 Apr), has an off-white to pale brownish cap, occasionally with yellowish or grey patches and often pitted or scarred. The white flesh is thick and firm, especially under the centre of the cap, and is said to smell of meal. The crowded off-white gills are small. The white stem is thick and fleshy, thicker at the base. The spores are white.

Edible and good; said to have hypoglycaemic properties. Discard the stem, slice thickly and steam or fry in oil or butter. Serve with Jersey royal potatoes and lots of parsley.

WHERE TO FIND

On grassland, including lawns and grass verges, especially when enriched with mushroom compost.

FACT FILE

FAMILY Lyophyllaceae CAP 5–11cm HEIGHT 3–9cm STATUS Widespread and common

JAN	FEB	MAR	APR	MAY	JUN	**JUL**	**AUG**	**SEP**	**OCT**	NOV	DEC

SHIMEJI

Lyophyllum decastes

WHERE TO FIND

In large dense clumps around tree stumps and on buried roots, usually in deciduous woodland.

The cap is greyish brown or reddish brown, large and fleshy with a wavy margin. The gills are off-white, crowded and wide. The thick, cylindrical stem is whitish, occasionally curved for better spore dispersal and fused with others at the base. The spores are white.

Although an alternative name (usually American) is the Fried Chicken Mushroom, most people agree that the flavour is nothing like that of fried chicken. This is one of a group of shimeji mushrooms cultivated commercially in Japan. Discard the stems and slice the caps horizontally. Toss them in butter and serve with ramen or soba noodles, beansprouts and bamboo shoots. The Latin epithet 'decastes' means 'a ten-man company of soldiers' and derives from the way this fungus grows in groups.

FACT FILE

FAMILY Tricholomataceae SYNONYMS Clustered Domecap, Fried Chicken Mushroom, *Tricholoma aggregatum* CAP 4–12cm HEIGHT 6–12cm STATUS Widespread POSSIBLE CONFUSION Similar to other brown-capped edible species, especially *L. fumosum* and *L. loricatum*. It must not be confused with the brown-capped *Entolomas*, so it is very important to ensure that the spores are not pink

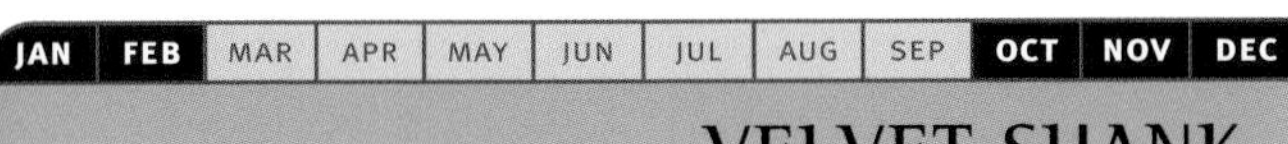

VELVET SHANK

Flammulina velutipes

The orange cap is hemispherical at first, flattening or becoming slightly depressed with age. It is paler at the edge, and smooth and sticky when wet. The off-white flesh is thin. The gills are creamy white at first, tending to redden when the fungus ages. Its most distinctive feature is the dark brown stem, which has the look and texture of velvet. It is tall and slender, narrowing towards the cap.

Grown commercially in the Far East, and known in Japan as Enokitake. Delicious in a fry-up with thinly sliced, fried potatoes and mangetouts.

WHERE TO FIND

Grows in clumps on rotting wood, especially the dead and diseased wood of deciduous trees. Look for it late in the year, even after a frost.

FACT FILE

FAMILY Physalacriaceae SYNONYM *Collybia velutipes* CAP 2–8cm HEIGHT 1–10cm STATUS Widespread

JAN	FEB	MAR	APR	MAY	**JUN**	**JUL**	**AUG**	**SEP**	**OCT**	NOV	DEC

PORCELAIN FUNGUS

Oudemansiella mucida

WHERE TO FIND

Grows exclusively on Beech *Fagus sylvatica*, in large numbers on the branches, trunk and stump.

It is a truly magnificent sight to look up into a Beech tree and see the light shining through this pure-white fungus. The cap is covered in a thick mucilage that makes it glisten, and it is translucent. It is always hemispherical but the edge may be wrinkled. The gills are widely spaced and the flesh is thin. There is always a prominent ring on the stem. The stem often curves to ensure that the cap remains parallel so the white spores are spread correctly.

Edible, once the mucilage is removed. Cook like Russet Toughshank (p. 33).

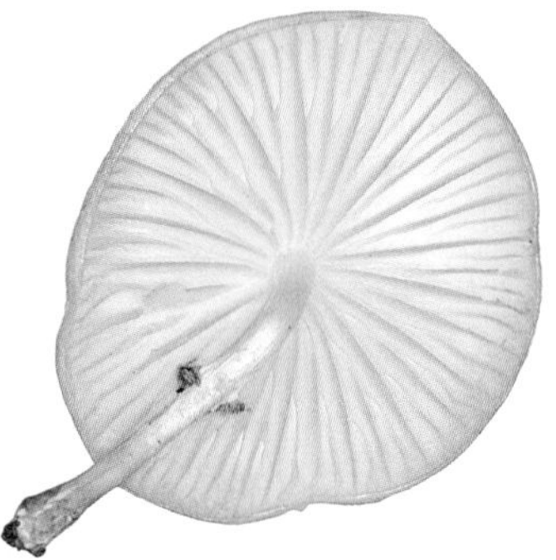

FACT FILE

FAMILY Physalacriaceae SYNONYM *Armillaria mucida* CAP 3–10cm HEIGHT 6–12cm
STATUS Widespread and common NOTE This species and the Pinecone Cap (p. 94) have been found to contain a powerful anti-fungal agent that is used on crops to protect against some plant diseases

THE DECEIVER

Laccaria laccata

The Deceiver is so called because of the wide variety of colours and forms it displays, but is recognisable by its overall shape and widely spaced, uneven gills. The cap is hemispherical at first, and may be various shades of brown, depending on the weather. The off-white flesh is thin. The gills are thick and flesh-coloured. The spores are white. The stem is tall and thin, and covered in short fibrils.

Discard the stems and fry in oil or butter, then serve on toast.

WHERE TO FIND

In soil under deciduous trees in woods, parks and on lawns.

FACT FILE

FAMILY Hydnangiaceae CAP 1–4cm HEIGHT 4–10cm STATUS Widespread and common POSSIBLE CONFUSION Wood Woollyfoot (p. 92) is similar but its stem is covered in long, pale hairs. May also be confused with Fairy Ring Champignon (p. 43)

JAN	FEB	MAR	APR	MAY	JUN	**JUL**	**AUG**	**SEP**	**OCT**	**NOV**	**DEC**

AMETHYST DECEIVER

Laccaria amethystina

WHERE TO FIND

In soil under deciduous trees, in woods, parks and on lawns.

Closely resembles The Deceiver (p. 41) but is entirely purple. The cap is hemispherical at first and often striated, with an irregular edge. The widely spaced gills are thick and the same colour as the cap. The spores are white. The stem is tall, thin and fragile. It is purple and covered in short white fibrils.

Cook like The Deceiver (p. 41).

FACT FILE

FAMILY Hydnangiaceae CAP 1–4cm HEIGHT 6–9cm STATUS Widespread and common POSSIBLE CONFUSION. Could be confused with poisonous purple species such as the Lilac Bonnet (p. 141) or Lilac Fibrecap *Inocybe geophylla* var. *lilacina*

FAIRY RING CHAMPIGNON

Marasmius oreades

The whole fungus is pale brown, darkening in wet weather. The cap is conical, with a marked central umbo that is usually darker than the remainder. The gills are pale brown, as is the flesh. The spores are white. The mycelium of this fungus grows outwards in a circle from a central point. The grass within the circle is often darker, since it is fertilised by the dead mycelium.

Edible, but the stems are tough. Delicious in an omelette, and suitable for drying.

WHERE TO FIND

Grows in groups in grassland, parks and gardens, often in rings or partial rings.

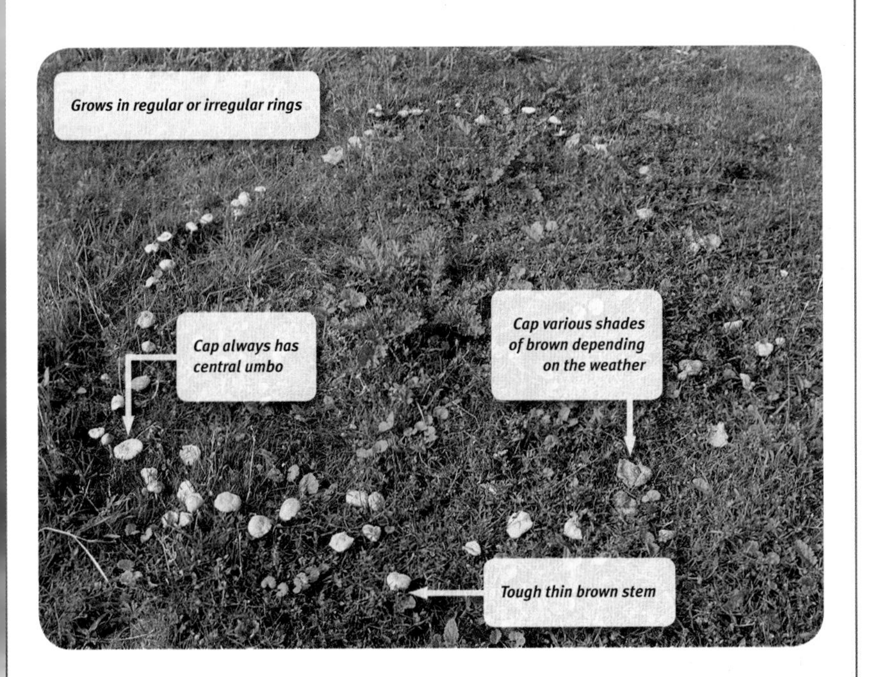

FACT FILE

FAMILY Marasmiaceae CAP 2–5cm HEIGHT 4–6cm STATUS Widespread and common POSSIBLE CONFUSION Similar to The Deceiver (p. 41), but that species (which is also edible) has a different habitat and does not grow in rings

JAN	FEB	MAR	APR	MAY	JUN	JUL	**AUG**	**SEP**	**OCT**	NOV	DEC

THE MILLER

Clitopilus prunulus

WHERE TO FIND

In mixed woods, among Heather *Erica vulgaris* and Bilberry *Vaccinum myrtillus.*

The cap is irregular in shape, remaining inrolled for a long time. It is white to pale brown, with a downy texture. The gills run down the stem and are crowded, turning pinkish as the pink spores mature. The flesh is thick but fragile, with a strong odour of meal. The white stem is thick and slightly swollen at the base, where it is covered in fluffy mycelium.

Edible but be wary of it, as The Miller resembles several poisonous all-white species.

FACT FILE

FAMILY Entolomataceae CAP 3–10cm HEIGHT 3–6cm STATUS Widespread
POSSIBLE CONFUSION Similar to many poisonous all-white species, so not recommended for novice mushroom hunters

JAN | FEB | MAR | **APR** | **MAY** | **JUN** | **JUL** | **AUG** | **SEP** | **OCT** | NOV | DEC

DEER SHIELD

Pluteus cervinus

The cap resembles the coat of a Fallow Deer (hence the species' common name), varying in colour from dark brown to fawn or light brown, and covered in fibrils. The edge of the cap remains inrolled for a long time. The flesh is soft, thin and white, and is said to smell faintly of radishes. The gills are white at first, turning pink when the pink spores mature, and are not attached to the stem. The tall, cylindrical stem is striped with longitudinal fibrils, these white at first, later turning brown.

Edible but of no value.

WHERE TO FIND

Occurs singly on heavily decayed wood and even on sawdust.

FACT FILE

FAMILY **Pluteaceae** SYNONYMS **Fawn Mushroom, Fawn Pluteus,** *Pluteus atricapillus* CAP **5–15cm** HEIGHT **5–10cm** STATUS **Widespread and common**

JAN	FEB	MAR	APR	MAY	JUN	**JUL**	**AUG**	**SEP**	**OCT**	**NOV**	**DEC**

STUBBLE ROSEGILL

Volvopluteus gloiocephalus

WHERE TO FIND

In grassland, stubble fields, wood chips and other places rich in organic matter, including compost heaps. It has a long growing season, lasting into winter, so may be found later in the year when other species have died off.

The genus *Volvopluteus* contains large, handsome species whose prominent volva at the base of the stem persists into maturity. The cap of the Stubble Rosegill is white to pale grey, ovoid at first, then domed and eventually flattening, but always with a central umbo. The flesh is white. The gills are pink and are not attached to the stem. The spores are pink. The tall, cylindrical white stem narrows at the top and is enclosed in a white volva at the base.

Edible but of no value.

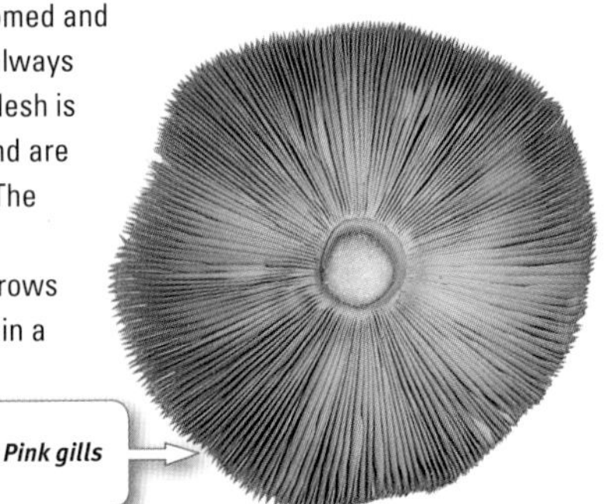

Pink gills

Cap retains central umbo even when old

Prominent volva sheaths the stem

FACT FILE

FAMILY Pluteaceae SYNONYMS *Volvariella gloiocephala, Volvaria gloiocephala* CAP 5–15cm HEIGHT 10–15cm STATUS Widespread NOTE In 2011 this species was reclassified into a separate genus as the result of DNA evidence

SILKY ROSEGILL

Volvariella bombycina

This is the handsomest of the rosegills. Its huge white cap is covered in glistening silky white fibrils. It does not flatten, remaining dome-shaped even when mature. The gills are pink and are not attached to the stem. The spores are pink. The tall, cylindrical white stem narrows at the top and is enclosed in a sac or volva at the base.

Edible and delicious, though should not be collected in Britain due to its rarity. Stew it with Asian vegetables.

WHERE TO FIND

Grows in small groups or singly, on rotting stumps and trunks of elms and Beech *Fagus sylvatica* or, occasionally, on other trees.

FACT FILE

FAMILY Pluteaceae SYNONYM *Volvaria bombycina* CAP 10–20cm HEIGHT 10–18cm STATUS Widespread but uncommon NOTE The related Paddy Straw Mushroom *V. volvacea* is a favourite edible fungus in South-East Asia

JAN FEB MAR APR MAY JUN **JUL AUG SEP OCT NOV** DEC

VIOLET WEBCAP

Cortinarius violaceus

This large, handsome *Cortinarius* is easily recognisable thanks to its all-purple coloration and the remains of the thin veil, or cortina, that remains attached to the cap, also creating a thin ring on the stem. The tall, cylindrical stem narrows at the top and swells at the base into a soft bulb. The thick flesh of both stem and cap is violet. The spores are rusty brown.

Edible but not good, and food cooked with it turns purple!

WHERE TO FIND

Grows singly or in groups in damp deciduous forests.

Thin veil (Cortina) or remains of veil hanging from cap margin

Bright purple coloration of whole fungus

FACT FILE

FAMILY Cortinariaceae CAP 5–12cm HEIGHT 6–12cm STATUS Widespread but uncommon
NOTE Most species in the genus *Cortinarius* are inedible and some are deadly poisonous

JAN FEB MAR **APR MAY JUN JUL AUG SEP OCT NOV** DEC

SHEATHED WOODTUFT

Kuehneromyces mutabilis

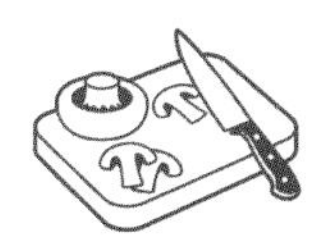

The smooth cap is honey-coloured in dry weather. It is pale ochre in the centre and darker at the edge – a distinctive feature. It is hemispherical at first, then expanding with a marked central umbo. The edge of the cap is thin and translucent. The gills are widely spaced and uneven, pale at first and then turning rust-coloured as the purple-brown spores ripen. The scaly yellow-brown stem, which is paler above the prominent ring, is often curved to ensure the cap is parallel to the ground for spore dispersal. The flesh is soft and cream-coloured under the cap.

Edible, except for the tough stem. Fry in butter with onions; needs a relatively long cooking time.

WHERE TO FIND

Grows in large tufts on the rotting wood of Beech *Fagus sylvatica* and other deciduous trees.

FACT FILE

FAMILY Strophariaceae SYNONYMS Changing Pholiota, *Pholiota mutabilis* CAP 3–8cm HEIGHT 4–10cm STATUS Widespread and common POSSIBLE CONFUSION Can be confused with the poisonous Funeral Bell (p. 145) and Sulphur Tuft (p. 152), and with the edible Honey Fungus *Armillaria mellea*

JAN	FEB	MAR	APR	MAY	JUN	JUL	**AUG**	**SEP**	**OCT**	**NOV**	DEC

GOLDEN SCALYCAP

Pholiota aurivella

The smooth cap is honey-coloured, darker in the centre and covered in prominent scales that remain the same colour throughout its life. It is hemispherical and slimy in wet weather. The flesh is yellow, pale brown in the base of the stem. The gills are yellow at first, becoming rust-coloured as the purple-brown spores ripen. The scaly yellow-brown stem has a faint ring two-thirds of the way up and is often curved to ensure the cap is parallel to the ground for spore dispersal.

Fry in oil or butter with a sprinkling of lemon juice.

WHERE TO FIND

Grows in large tufts on the rotting wood of Beech *Fagus sylvatica* and other deciduous trees.

Domed golden cap is dotted with occasional flattened scales

FACT FILE

FAMILY Strophariaceae CAP 4–15cm HEIGHT 5–7.5cm STATUS Widespread
POSSIBLE CONFUSION The similar Shaggy Scalycap (p. 153) is poisonous; its scales are much darker, denser and shaggier

JAN	FEB	MAR	APR	MAY	**JUN**	**JUL**	**AUG**	**SEP**	**OCT**	**NOV**	DEC

SCALY WOOD MUSHROOM

Agaricus langei

The whitish cap of this large mushroom is densely covered in rust-coloured scales, especially in the centre. The thick white stem tapers upwards and in mature specimens is encircled by a large floppy ring. The flesh is white, staining red when the mushroom is cut or bruised. The crowded gills are pink at first, darkening as the purple-brown spores ripen.

Cook in the same way as you would any shop-bought mushroom.

UPPERSIDE.

WHERE TO FIND

On soil, mainly in coniferous woods, and occasionally in deciduous woods.

FACT FILE

FAMILY Agaricaceae SYNONYM *Psalliota langei* CAP 4–12cm HEIGHT 5–12cm STATUS Widespread but uncommon POSSIBLE CONFUSION Similar to other members of the genus, which also includes the poisonous Yellow Stainer (p. 154)

JAN	FEB	MAR	APR	MAY	**JUN**	**JUL**	**AUG**	**SEP**	**OCT**	NOV	DEC

FIELD MUSHROOM

Agaricus campestris

WHERE TO FIND

A grassland species found in abundance in meadows, lawns and parks. Look for it after rain following a long dry spell.

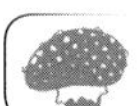

The Field Mushroom is closely related to the Cultivated Mushroom *A. bisporus* – only microscopic characteristics definitively tell them apart. It generally has a thick, fleshy white cap with a ragged edge, although in one variety the cap is covered in small brown scales. The remains of the veil form a ring on the thick white stem. The flesh is white, staining slightly pink when the mushroom is cut or bruised. The narrow gills are pink at first, darkening as the purple-brown spores ripen.

Edible and delicious; safe to eat raw. Use in the same way as any shop-bought mushroom, including for making soup.

Cap white or covered in brown scales, always domed

Pink gills darkening to purple-brown when mature

Ring present, faint or absent

No volva at base

FACT FILE

FAMILY Agaricaceae SYNONYM *Psalliota campestris* CAP 4–10cm HEIGHT 3–10cm STATUS Widespread and common POSSIBLE CONFUSION Similar to other members of the genus, which includes the poisonous Yellow Stainer (p. 154)

HORSE MUSHROOM

Agaricus arvensis

In grassland, including lawns and parks. Also, in open woodland.

The cap is thick, fleshy and white, often with a brown patch in the centre. It is smooth and sticky in wet weather, and in dry weather may crack and appear scaly. The remains of the veil form a floppy ring on the thick white stem. The flesh is white, staining faintly yellow when the mushroom is cut or bruised. The narrow gills are pink at first, darkening as the purple-brown spores ripen.

Edible and delicious; sometimes flavoured with a hint of aniseed. Cook as you would any shop-bought mushroom.

FACT FILE

FAMILY Agaricaceae SYNONYM *Psalliota arvensis* CAP 5–15cm HEIGHT 8–12cm STATUS Widespread and common POSSIBLE CONFUSION Other members of the genus are similar, including the poisonous Yellow Stainer (p. 154)

JAN FEB MAR APR MAY **JUN JUL AUG SEP OCT NOV** DEC

WOOD MUSHROOM

Agaricus silvicola

WHERE TO FIND

Grows in groups on rich soil in deciduous and coniferous woods.

The silky white cap is hemispherical at first, flattening with age, and is occasionally stained with yellow patches, especially so when bruised. As in all members of the *Agaricus* genus, the cap peels easily. The remains of the veil form a floppy ring on the tall white stem, which ends in a bulb. The thick flesh is white, staining faintly yellow when the mushroom is cut. The gills are crowded, pink at first and darkening to brownish black as the purple-brown spores ripen.

Edible and delicious. Cook in the same way as you would any shop-bought mushroom.

FACT FILE

FAMILY Agaricaceae SYNONYM *Psalliota silvicola* CAP 7–14cm HEIGHT 5–12cm STATUS Widespread POSSIBLE CONFUSION Similar to other members of the genus, including the poisonous Yellow Stainer (p. 154)

SHAGGY INKCAP

Coprinus comatus

This very distinctive mushroom has an ovoid cap that never expands. It is thickly covered in shaggy white scales, except at the very top, where there is a large brown scale. The flesh is white, and the long, crowded gills are pink when young. As the fungus matures, the margin turns black from the black spores and the whole fungus dissolves into a liquid, a process known as deliquescence. The sturdy white stem, which has a thin white ring, does not deliquesce.

Edible only when young, before it starts to deliquesce. Sauté in butter with onions or shallots.

WHERE TO FIND

In soil, including borders, park, lawns and grass verges especially in places that have been disturbed.

FACT FILE

FAMILY Agaricaceae SYNONYM Lawyer's Wig CAP 2–6cm HEIGHT 10–20cm STATUS Widespread and common

JAN	FEB	MAR	APR	MAY	**JUN**	**JUL**	**AUG**	**SEP**	**OCT**	**NOV**	DEC

WEEPING WIDOW

Lacrymaria lacrymabunda

WHERE TO FIND

On grassland in groups and clumps, sometimes with several stems fused together at a single point.

The cap is bell-shaped at first, becoming hemispherical with age but retaining a central umbo. It is brown, sometimes with ochre patches, and is covered in brown scales that give it a velvety appearance. The flesh is thin, firm and pale brown. The crowded brown gills are edged with white and exude clear droplets like tears, hence the species' name. They darken as the black spores mature. The tall, hollow stem is white, but covered in brown fibrils except immediately under the cap.

Edible with caution when young. Cook in a little butter and serve with mashed or fried potatoes.

FACT FILE

FAMILY Psathyrellaceae SYNONYMS *Lacrymaria velutina, Psathyrella lacrymabunda* CAP 3–7cm HEIGHT 6–9cm STATUS Widespread and common POSSIBLE CONFUSION Small brown fungi – including inedible and poisonous species – all look very similar and so should not be eaten by novice mushroom hunters

PALE BRITTLESTEM

Psathyrella candolleana

The cap is creamy white or ochre, ovoid at first and then flattening. There is a small central umbo that is light brown to bright yellow. The remains of a veil sometimes hang from the edge, which becomes ragged and turns black as the spores mature. The crowded gills are pinkish grey, turning dark from the black spores. The tall white stem is hollow and brittle, and sometimes enlarges into a bulb at the foot, which is covered in white mycelium. The thin flesh is greyish and watery.

Edible and said to have medicinal properties. The flesh is thin, so best served in a soup.

WHERE TO FIND

Grows in large groups on rotten wood and on grass verges.

FACT FILE

FAMILY Psathyrellaceae
SYNONYM Crumble Tuft
CAP 3–6cm HEIGHT 4–7cm
STATUS Widespread and common

JAN	FEB	MAR	APR	MAY	**JUN**	**JUL**	**AUG**	**SEP**	**OCT**	**NOV**	DEC

GLISTENING INKCAP

Coprinellus micaceus

WHERE TO FIND

Grows in dense clusters that may be welded together, at the base of the stem on rotting wood in woodland.

The egg-shaped cap is light brown to ochre, paler at the top. It is striated and and is initially covered in shiny specks that glisten like mica, hence its name. The margin becomes ragged in older specimens as it starts to deliquesce. The crowded gills are off-white when young, turning brown as the black spores mature. The thin brown flesh has no taste or smell. The thin white stem lacks a ring.

Edible and considered delicious by some people, but it is very friable and the flavour is mild. Eat it in omelettes and other egg dishes, or fry it in butter and sprinkle over a baked pasta dish.

Cap topped with a few shiny scales

Brown bell-shaped cap covered in ridges except at the top

Grows in large numbers, sometimes welded together

FACT FILE

FAMILY Psathyrellaceae
SYNONYM *Coprinus micaceus*
CAP 3–7cm HEIGHT 5–15cm
STATUS Widespread and common
POSSIBLE CONFUSION The Hare's Foot Inkcap *Coprinopsis lagopus* is similar, with a greyish to brown partial coating of scales on the pleated silvery cap. However, its stem is downy and lacks a ring

OYSTER MUSHROOM

Pleurotus ostreatus

The growth habit and shape of this delicious fungus make it highly distinctive. The oval cap is a shiny metallic grey. The stem is eccentric, forming part of the white underside of the cap, or is missing altogether. The crowded gills, spores and thick flesh are all white.

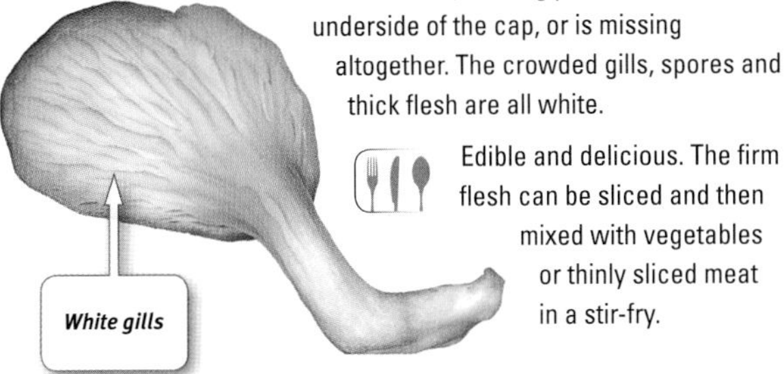

Edible and delicious. The firm flesh can be sliced and then mixed with vegetables or thinly sliced meat in a stir-fry.

WHERE TO FIND

Large numbers of imbricated caps grow on the trunks and branches of dead or dying deciduous trees, mainly Beech *Fagus sylvatica*, poplars and oaks.

FACT FILE

FAMILY Pleurotaceae CAP 6–15cm HEIGHT 3–5cm STATUS Widespread and common POSSIBLE CONFUSION A similar species, whose cap is bluer, is known as the Blue Oyster Mushroom *P. columbinus*; it is found on pine. The Elm Leech *Hypsizygus ulmarius* also looks similar but its cap is brown and it grows exclusively on elms

JAN FEB MAR APR MAY JUN **JUL AUG SEP OCT NOV** DEC

VEILED OYSTER

Pleurotus dyrinus

The greyish or off-white cap is almost circular, making the species look more like a bracket fungus. The cap is covered in felty scales when young but these disappear as the fungus matures, and the edge sometimes has wisps of a veil hanging from it. The flesh is thick and white. The stem is long and thick for an oyster mushroom, eccentric and deeply embedded in the wood. The gills are crowded and white, running down the stem. The spores are white.

Edible when young. Cook in the same way as Oyster Mushroom (p. 59).

WHERE TO FIND

Grows on the trunks and branches of many deciduous trees, especially oaks; also found rarely on conifers.

FACT FILE

FAMILY Pleurotaceae SYNONYM Oak Oyster
CAP 6–15cm HEIGHT 3–5cm
STATUS Widespread and common

ROSY SPIKE

Gomphidius roseus

The members of the *Gomphidius* genus have a very distinctive outline. The slimy cap and the stem merge into each other and are all of a piece. In the Rosy Spike, the cap is bright red to pink, with small, widely spaced gills running down the stem. The cap is convex at first, flattening slightly later. The flesh is whitish but red under the cap. The gills are white at first, turning grey.

Edible with caution. Cook in butter or oil with onion and a sprig of thyme.

WHERE TO FIND

Under pine trees and in clearings. Often grows in association with the Bovine Bolete *Suillus bovinus*, so if you come across that species look for Rosy Spike nearby.

FACT FILE

FAMILY Gomphidiaceae CAP 3–6cm HEIGHT 3–6cm STATUS Widespread and common POSSIBLE CONFUSION May be mistaken for many other small red-capped species

JAN FEB MAR APR MAY JUN **JUL AUG SEP OCT** NOV DEC

CHANTERELLE

Cantharellus cibarius

WHERE TO FIND

Grows in large troops, in association with both deciduous and coniferous trees. Look for Chanterelles after rain, when they fruit.

These distinctive funnel-shaped fungi have thick veins under the cap in place of gills – a distinctive feature. The cap and stem are all of a piece. The whole fungus is a bright orange-yellow. The thick flesh is white, as are the spores.

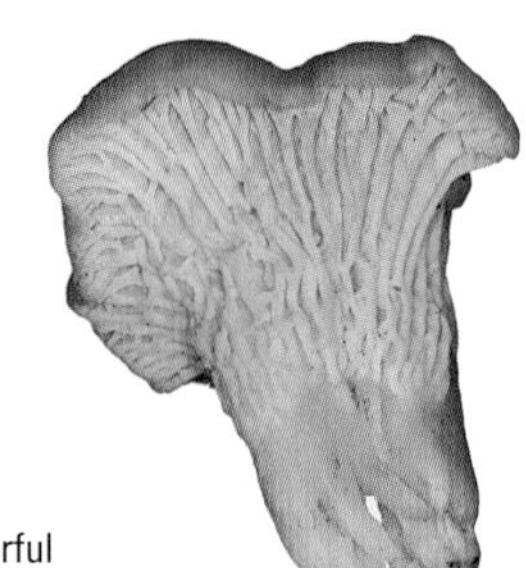

Edible and delicious. Wonderful with scrambled eggs or in a stir-fry.

FACT FILE

FAMILY Cantharellaceae CAP 5–10cm HEIGHT 6–13cm STATUS Widespread and common
POSSIBLE CONFUSION The False Chanterelle (p. 84) bears some resemblance to the Chanterelle but it has true gills. It is inedible

HORN OF PLENTY

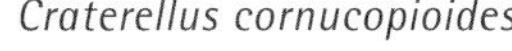

Craterellus cornucopioides

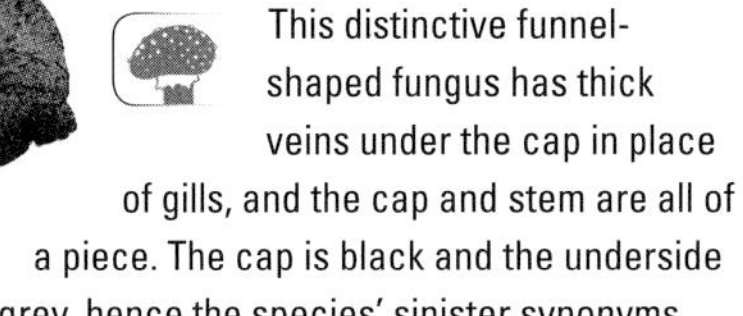

This distinctive funnel-shaped fungus has thick veins under the cap in place of gills, and the cap and stem are all of a piece. The cap is black and the underside is grey, hence the species' sinister synonyms. Nevertheless, it is perfectly good to eat.

Edible and delicious. Cook like the Chanterelle (p. 62).

Underside of cap has veins instead of gills

WHERE TO FIND

Grows in large numbers under both deciduous and coniferous trees, especially amongst moss.

FACT FILE

FAMILY Cantharellaceae SYNONYMS Black Chanterelle, Black Trumpet, Trumpet of the Dead CAP 5–10cm HEIGHT 6–13cm STATUS Widespread and common

JAN	FEB	MAR	APR	MAY	JUN	JUL	**AUG**	**SEP**	**OCT**	**NOV**	**DEC**

WINTER CHANTERELLE

Craterellus tubaeformis

WHERE TO FIND

Grows mainly beneath spruce and pine trees, on damp mossy or leaf litter-covered soil. Fruiting bodies persist beyond the first frosts.

A funnel-shaped fungus with a pale greyish cap and bright yellow stipe. When mature, the cap is wavy-edged and irregular, with prominent pale veins rather than gills on the underside. These branch out from the top of the stipe; the cap and stipe blend together without a clear dividing line. The stipe sometimes shows a long, vertical indentation. Difficult to spot, but often grows in dense clusters. Has a sweet fruity smell.

Edible, with pleasant earthy flavour. Best roasted or fried and paired with rich creamy sauces.

FACT FILE

FAMILY **Cantharellaceae** SYNONYMS **Yellowfoot, Winter Mushroom** CAP **3–7cm** HEIGHT **8–9cm** STATUS **Common and widespread** POSSIBLE CONFUSION **Similar to Chanterelle (p. 62) but with a pale whitish or yellowish-grey cap and bright yellow stipe.**

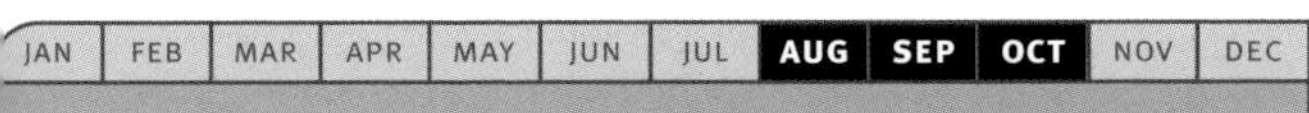

COMMON PUFFBALL

Lycoperdon perlatum

This all-white puffball is pestle-shaped, its pseudo-stem topped with a bulbous head covered in tiny conical spines or warts. The flesh is white and spongy when the fungus is immature, but turns yellow-brown to olive and powdery as the spores mature; at this stage a ragged hole opens in the top and the spores drift out into the wind.

Edible only when young, before the spores mature. Slice it and fry it in oil or butter and serve with eggs. Used in French folk medicine as a styptic and to aid digestion.

WHERE TO FIND

In woodlands and wood chips, growing singly and in groups.

FACT FILE

FAMILY Agaricaceae HEAD DIAMETER 3–5cm HEIGHT 3–9cm STATUS Widespread and common

JAN	FEB	MAR	APR	MAY	JUN	**JUL**	**AUG**	**SEP**	**OCT**	NOV	DEC

GIANT PUFFBALL

Calvatia gigantea

WHERE TO FIND

In nutrient enriched grassland and parks, growing in groups.

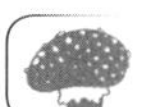

This all-white puffball is almost certainly one of the largest fungi in the world (a specimen found in Hungary weighed 20kg). It resembles a human skull lying on its side, hence its scientific name. The flesh is white and spongy when the fungus is immature, but turns yellow-brown to olive and powdery as the spores mature. At this stage the outer skin breaks up exposing the spore mass to the wind.

Edible only when young, before the spores mature. Cook in the same way as Common Puffball (p. 65).

FACT FILE

FAMILY Agaricaceae SYNONYM *Langermannia gigantea*
DIAMETER 30cm or more STATUS Widespread and common

GREY PUFFBALL

Bovista plumbea

Unlike other puffballs, this small grey fungus is not securely anchored to the ground and is tossed about in the wind when it matures. It is completely round and is white when young, later turning grey. The outer skin flakes away to reveal the silvery-grey skin inside, which contains the yellow-brown to olive powdery spores.

Edible only when immature and the spores are white, and should be eaten on the day of picking to prevent it maturing. Like all puffballs, the flesh should be sliced thinly and fried in oil or butter. The slices can then be added to pasta dishes or eaten with cooked beans.

WHERE TO FIND

In grassland and parks, and on grass verges, growing singly and in groups.

FACT FILE

FAMILY Agaricaceae SYNONYM Leaden Puffball
DIAMETER 2.5–3.5cm STATUS Widespread and common

JAN FEB MAR APR MAY JUN JUL AUG SEP OCT NOV DEC

DRYAD'S SADDLE

Polyporus squamosus

WHERE TO FIND

Grows on deciduous trees, mainly oaks. Can be found year-round but puts out new caps in early summer, which is the best time to collect it for the table.

Grows in groups, the large caps usually piled on top of one another. The cap is kidney-shaped and covered in concentric orange-brown to dark ochre scales on a smooth beige ground. The stem is eccentric or non-existent, so that the caps often grow straight out of the trunk. The underside is cream-coloured and covered in angular pores. The white flesh is firm when young, leathery in older specimens.

Edible when young, but requires long cooking to tenderise it. Slice it very thinly and sauté slowly in butter, then add to bean or meat stews.

Grows on deciduous trees

FACT FILE

FAMILY Polyporaceae SYNONYM *Melanopus squamosus* CAP 20–70cm HEIGHT 3–10cm STATUS Widespread and common

Cap covered in orange-brown to ochre scales

Underside covered in white pores

Usually in clumps with imbricated caps

CHICKEN OF THE WOODS

Laetiporus sulphureus

This polypore is unmistakable thanks to its brilliant colour. It forms superimposed lobed brackets, which grow straight out of one side of the host tree. The upper surface of the brackets is a brilliant sulphur-yellow or orange, sometimes with a wide yellow band at the margin. The flesh is white at first, tending to yellow with age. The underside, bearing the pores, is bright yellow.

Edible and delicious when young. Slice thinly as the brackets are tough. Stew in butter for at least 10 minutes in a covered saucepan.

WHERE TO FIND

Parasitises deciduous or coniferous trees, continuing to live on them after it has killed them; also found on dead stumps.

FACT FILE

FAMILY Polyporaceae SYNONYMS Sulphur Polypore, *Polyporus sulphureus*
DIAMETER 15–20cm THICKNESS 0.5–2cm STATUS Widespread and common

JAN | FEB | MAR | APR | MAY | JUN | JUL | AUG | SEP | OCT | NOV | DEC

HAIRY BRACKET

Trametes hirsuta

WHERE TO FIND

Causes white rot in deciduous trees, especially birches and Beech *Fagus sylvatica.*

The fruiting body grows in thick single or overlapping groups. The irregular upper surface is whitish to yellow-brown when young, greying with age, and is covered in silvery hairs arranged in concentric rings. The flesh is white, tough and leathery, so eat the species only when young. The pores are round and cream-coloured.

Slice thinly and sauté in oil or butter.

White flesh and pores

Covered in silvery 'hairs' arranged in concentric rings

FACT FILE

FAMILY **Polyporaceae** SYNONYMS **Hirsute Polypore,** *Coriolus hirsutus*
DIAMETER **2–10cm** STATUS **Widespread but uncommon**

WOOD CAULIFLOWER

Sparassis crispa

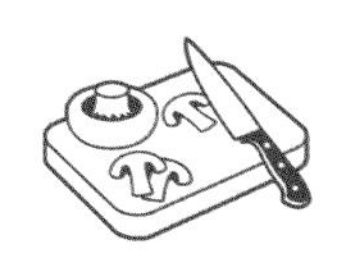

This handsome, distinctive fungus looks a little like a frisée or Batavia lettuce. It grows from a single stem, branching into numerous flattened, incurving whitish or yellowish lobed branches with ragged edges that carry the white spores. It is unmistakable.

Edible and delicious but requires careful cleaning. Toss it in butter and add it to vegetable dishes or a stew.

WHERE TO FIND

Grows at the base of pine trees, and on pine wood chips where it forms an association with the roots of the tree.

INSET: *PORES.*

FACT FILE

FAMILY Sparassidaceae DIAMETER <40cm STATUS Widespread but uncommon
POSSIBLE CONFUSION *S. spathulata* (also known as *S. laminosa*), which some authorities believe merely to be a variety of *S. crispa*, grows at the foot of oak and other deciduous trees. It is also edible

JAN	FEB	MAR	APR	**MAY**	**JUN**	**JUL**	**AUG**	**SEP**	OCT	NOV	DEC

JELLY TOOTH

Pseudohydnum gelatinosum

WHERE TO FIND

Grows on dead conifer wood.

The fan- or spade-shaped bluish-grey lumps of this fungus have a jelly-like consistency, and like all jelly fungi vary in shape. The flesh is gelatinous, shrinking or swelling depending on the atmospheric humidity. The brownish upper surface is downy, and the underside is covered in off-white spines on which the white spores are carried.

Edible but cannot be dried. Cook it in soups with Asian vegetables.

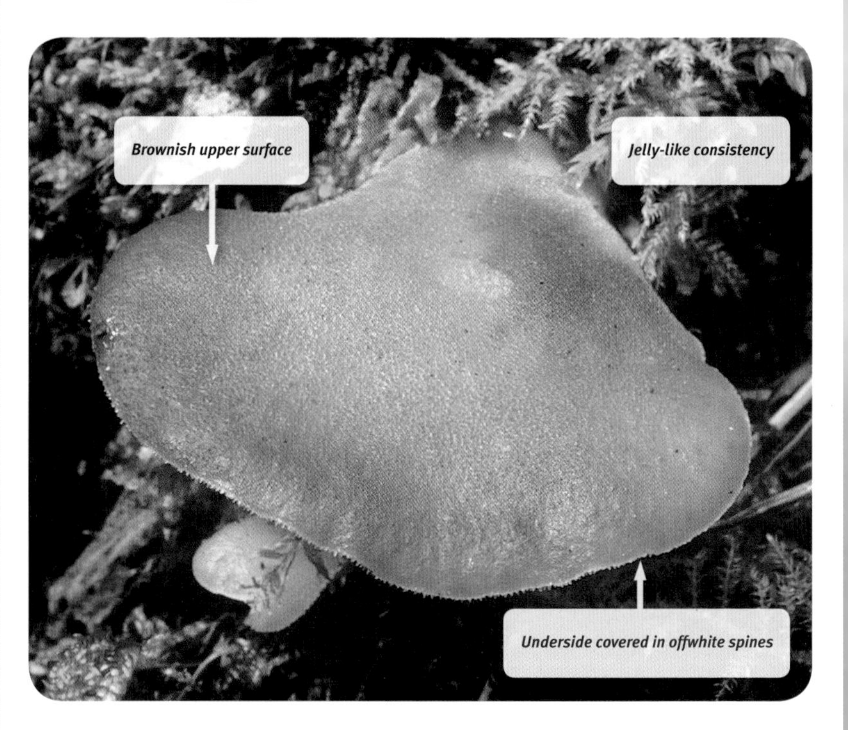

FACT FILE

FAMILY Exidiaceae SYNONYMS Toothed Jelly Fungus, False Hedgehog Mushroom, White Jelly Mushroom, *Tremellodon gelatinosum* DIAMETER 2–6cm THICKNESS 1–3cm STATUS Widespread but uncommon

GIANT POLYPORE

Meripilus giganteus

This polypore forms massive superimposed brackets that are welded laterally at the base in a deformed stump or pseudo-stem. The upper surface of the brackets is covered in sepia to paler brown concentric rings. The flesh is white at first, turning darker and eventually blackening. The underside, bearing the pores, is white, darkening when cut.

Edible when young. The caps are tough, so need slow stewing in oil or butter in a saucepan with a tight-fitting lid.

WHERE TO FIND

Fruits in large numbers mainly at the foot of dead or dying Beech *Fagus sylvatica* and less frequently other deciduous trees.

FACT FILE

FAMILY Meripilaceae SYNONYM *Polyporus giganteus* DIAMETER <2m THICKNESS 0.5–2cm STATUS Widespread and common

JAN FEB MAR APR MAY JUN JUL AUG SEP OCT NOV DEC

BENZOIN BRACKET

Ischnoderma benzoinum

WHERE TO FIND

Grows singly or in a few overlapping brackets on logs and stumps of coniferous trees.

The thick bracket is rounded at first, expanding into a semicircular shape with a lobed margin. It exudes a resin from the smooth, felty, dark rusty-brown to black zoned surface. The margin is whitish, sometimes with a raised rim that covers the pores at the edge of the white underside. The crowded tubes end in small round pores. The flesh is elastic at first, becoming hard in mature specimens, and is off-white like the spores.

Slice thinly and sauté in oil or butter.

FACT FILE

FAMILY Fomitopsidaceae DIAMETER 1–15cm
THICKNESS 0.5–2cm STATUS Widespread and uncommon

CONFLUENT SHEEP POLYPORE

Albatrellus confluens

This unusual polypore grows on the ground and has a characteristic mushroom shape, although it has tiny pores instead of gills. It has a pale orange cap with a creamy-white undersurface, although the cap may be covered in green algae. The flesh is white and soft at first, tending to stain greenish or yellow with age. The underside, bearing the pores, is bright yellow. The stem is usually slightly off-centre. It is off-white and may develop tan or green discolorations.

Edible when young. Cook as for Chicken of the Woods (p. 69). Can be dried, when it turns red.

Found in large numbers under conifers, growing on the ground.

FACT FILE

FAMILY Albatrellaceae SYNONYM *Polyporus confluens*
CAP 3–20cm, HEIGHT 3–6cm STATUS Widespread but uncommon

JAN	FEB	MAR	**APR**	**MAY**	**JUN**	**JUL**	**AUG**	**SEP**	**OCT**	NOV	DEC

GREY POLYPORE

Boletopsis grisea

WHERE TO FIND

Grows in association with the Scots Pine *Pinus sylvestris*.

Although this fungus grows on the ground, has pores and is mushroom-shaped, it is not a true bolete and belongs to a different family. The cap surface is grey, undulating and irregular in shape. The underside is white and covered in tiny pores. The thick stalk is greyish.

Edible when young but the tough stalk must be discarded. In Japan, where it is known as the Kurotake, it is believed to have medicinal properties and is dried and made into a tea.

FACT FILE

FAMILY Bankeraceae SYNONYMS *Polyporus griseus*, *Boletopsis subsquamosa*, Kurotake CAP 4–8cm HEIGHT 5–10cm STATUS Widespread and common NOTE *B. leucomelaena*, once classed as a separate species, is now considered a variety of Grey Polypore

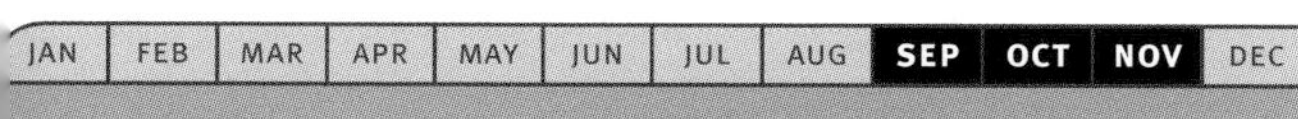

BEARDED TOOTH

Hericium erinaceus

The massive cream or white cap or head is virtually spherical, growing from a single short stem. It is entirely covered in tightly packed spines as long as 4cm, which themselves are covered by the spore-bearing layer. The flesh is gelatinous when young and leathery when old, when the colour of the fungus darkens to light brown.

Edible only when young. Said to have hypoglycaemic properties. The tough flesh should be cooked like that of Chicken of the Woods (p. 69).

WHERE TO FIND

A single huge mass, growing on standing and fallen trunks of deciduous trees especially Beech *Fagus sylvatica*.

Whole fungus pure white, yellowing and browning with age

Grows in one large clump

INSET: *PORES.*

FACT FILE

FAMILY Hericaceae SYNONYMS Lion's Mane, Monkey Head, *Dryodon erinaceum*, *Hydnum erinaceum*. DIAMETER 10–24cm STATUS Widespread but uncommon POSSIBLE CONFUSION The Coral Tooth *H. coralloides* has a similar habitat and general shape, and is also edible. NOTE The species is protected in several European countries, including the UK and Sweden

JAN | FEB | MAR | APR | MAY | JUN | **JUL** | **AUG** | **SEP** | **OCT** | NOV | DEC

BEEFSTEAK FUNGUS

Fistulina hepatica

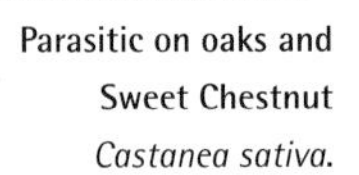

WHERE TO FIND

Parasitic on oaks and Sweet Chestnut *Castanea sativa.*

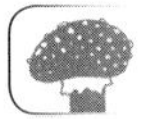

Starting as a small red knob on the side of the host tree, the Beefsteak Fungus expands into a bracket- or tongue-shaped excrescence that is entirely distinctive. The slimy, dark red covering on the cap is easily separated from the flesh, and is covered in small papillae like a human or animal tongue. The tubes containing the spores are yellow at first, turning red, and are attached to each other but separable. The stem is short or absent.

Edible when young, even raw. Popular in salads, cooked or raw, but first peel off and discard the slimy coating.

MAIN PIC: *UPPERSIDE;* INSET: *UNDERSIDE.*

FACT FILE

FAMILY **Fistulinaceae** DIAMETER **6–25cm.** THICKNESS **2–6cm** STATUS **Widespread and common**

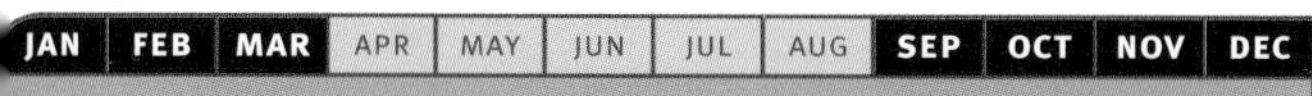

YELLOW BRAIN

Tremella mesenterica

The fruit body is a slimy orange-yellow mass that is very convoluted and folded, so that it looks like brain tissue – hence the species' common name. It flattens and desiccates in dry weather, becoming tough and leathery, but swells again immediately after rain. Some varieties are olive-green and even white.

Edible and said to have medicinal properties. Because of its gelatinous consistency, it is best eaten in a soup with Asian vegetables.

WHERE TO FIND

On the branches of dead and dying deciduous trees, as a parasite of fungi in the genus *Peniophora*.

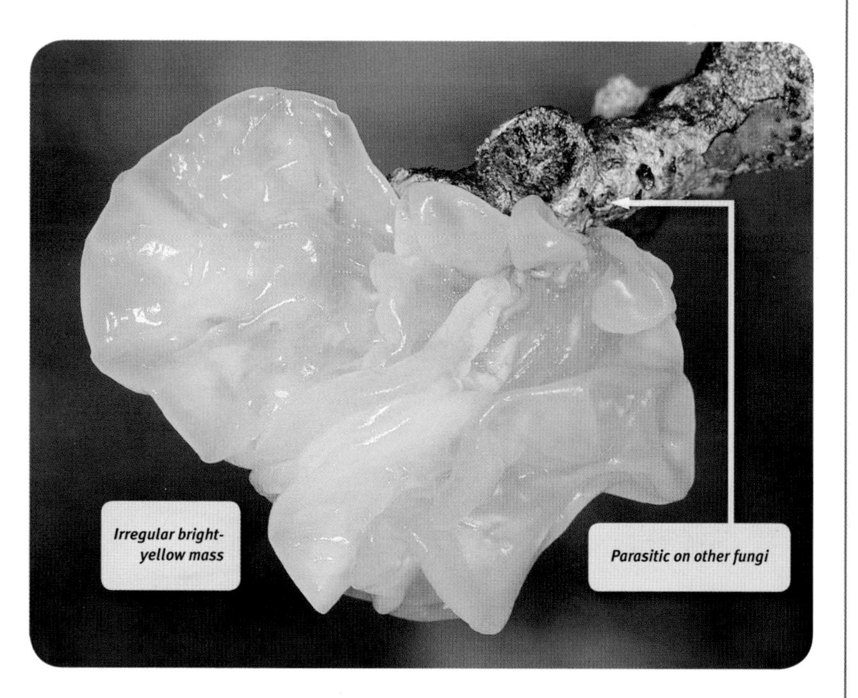

FACT FILE

FAMILY Tremellaceae SYNONYM Witches' Butter (do not confuse with the inedible *Exidia glandulosa*, p. 129) HEIGHT 2–5cm STATUS Widespread and common POSSIBLE CONFUSION May be confused with other jelly fungi such as the Leafy Brain *T. foliacea*, but that species is reddish brown

JAN | FEB | MAR | APR | MAY | JUN | JUL | AUG | SEP | OCT | NOV | DEC

JELLY EAR

Auricularia auricula-judae

WHERE TO FIND

Said to grow exclusively on Elder *Sambucus nigra*, but found on other deciduous trees, including Hazel *Corylus avellana*; occurs in clusters.

The fruit body is indeed ear-shaped, being thin, lobed and veined. The stem is short or absent. The outer surface is velvety in appearance and the whole fungus is translucent. The colour may be greyish brown or even greenish, but is more typically brick-red. The inner, spore-bearing surface is shiny.

Edible and delicious, and can be eaten raw. The closely related Cloud Ear *A. polytricha* is much used in Chinese cooking; both species are eaten in soups and salads.

FACT FILE

FAMILY Auriculariaceae SYNONYMS Wood Ear, Jew's Ear, *Hirneola auricula-judae* HEIGHT 2–5cm STATUS Widespread and common POSSIBLE CONFUSION May be confused with other jelly fungi such as the reddish-brown Leafy Brain *Tremella foliacea* NOTE The scientific species name is a shortened version of 'Judas ear', as Judas Iscariot is said to have hanged himself on an Elder tree. The fungus can freeze solid and recover quickly, and actually produces spores in the coldest months of the year

JAN | FEB | MAR | APR | MAY | JUN | **JUL** | **AUG** | **SEP** | **OCT** | **NOV** | **DEC**

WOOD HEDGEHOG

Hydnum repandum

Members of the genus *Hydnum* have the classic mushroom shape but the underside of the cap is covered in tiny spines that bear the spores. The cap of the Wood Hedgehog is smooth to finely velvety and cream-coloured, and is often pitted, irregular and lumpy. The spine-bearing undersurface is white, as is the thick flesh. The stem is thick, white and short, often shorter than the diameter of the cap.

Edible, especially when young. Fry it with onions or shallots. The thick, firm flesh can be sliced and dried.

WHERE TO FIND

Grows in large numbers, sometimes in rings, in mixed woodlands at low altitude. Persists well into the winter, as it can withstand temperatures as low as –5˚C, so this may be a good time to seek it out.

FACT FILE

FAMILY **Hydnaceae** DIAMETER **5–10cm**
STATUS **Widespread and common**

JAN	FEB	**MAR**	**APR**	**MAY**	**JUN**	JUL	AUG	SEP	OCT	NOV	DEC

FALSE MOREL

Gyromitra esculenta

WHERE TO FIND

Grows in small groups on the ground mainly under conifers, with a preference for pines on sandy soil. One of the few spring fungi.

The cap is large and wide, irregular and swollen in relation to the stem, with many brain-like folds. It is dark reddish brown or sepia, with an inner surface that is white like the stem. The stem is thick but hollow, folded and furrowed, and may turn light brown with age.

Despite the epithet *esculenta*, meaning 'edible', this fungus is suspect and must not be eaten raw. Must be thoroughly cooked. Parboil it, then fry and eat with fried potatoes.

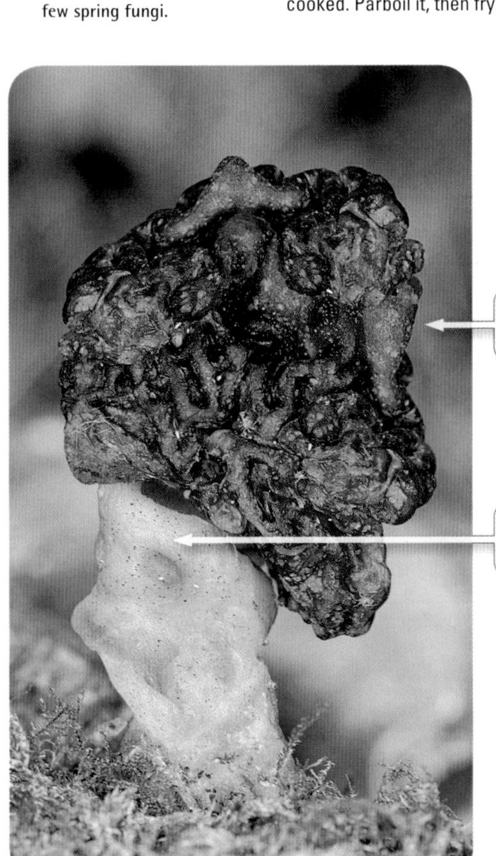

FACT FILE

FAMILY Discinaceae DIAMETER 10–15cm HEIGHT 4–6cm STATUS Widespread but uncommon POSSIBLE CONFUSION The Morel (p. 83) is also found in spring and its cap is similar in shape, but like the true morels the cap is pitted and alveolate as well as folded

MOREL

Morchella esculenta

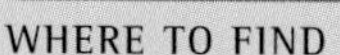

In damp woods, parks and gardens, on sandy soil and in burnt places.

The Morel is considered to be one of the finest edible mushrooms and has been compared to the Black Truffle *Tuber melanosporum* for its delicious flavour. It grows in Spring, and although it appears to have a cap and pseudo-stem, it is not related to the gill fungi but is an ascomycete, its spores growing inside small sacs known as asci. The cap, which is covered in pits or alveoles, is grey-brown and ovoid or round. The pseudo-stem is white, irregular, furrowed and pitted. There are a few other close relatives of the Morel that have a very similar appearance and are equally delicious, notably *Morchella elata*.

Edible and delicious. Makes an excellent stuffing if mixed with breadcrumbs, ground almonds, seasonings and parsley, for poultry or rolled and boned breast of lamb or veal. Or stew it in butter and serve as an accompaniment like a vegetable. Can also be dried.

FACT FILE

FAMILY Morchellaceae
SYNONYM *M. vulgaris*
CAP 3–7cm
HEIGHT 5–15cm
STATUS Widespread but uncommon

Deeply pitted dark brown 'cap'

Short thick white 'stem'

JAN	FEB	MAR	APR	MAY	**JUN**	**JUL**	**AUG**	**SEP**	**OCT**	NOV	DEC

FALSE CHANTERELLE

Hygrophoropsis aurantiaca

The cap is convex and inrolled at first but eventually develops into a funnel shape. It is orange-yellow in colour. The thin, smooth, fibrous stem narrows at the base and is concolorous or darker than the cap. The crowded gills are orange-red to yellow and run down the stem. The spores are white.

WHERE TO FIND

Grows in small groups on rotting wood on the ground in coniferous forests, mainly pine and spruce.

FACT FILE

FAMILY Hygrophoropsidaceae CAP 3–7cm HEIGHT 3–10cm STATUS Widespread and common POSSIBLE CONFUSION Similar to the Chanterelle (p. 62) but that species does not have gills

PARASITIC BOLETE

Pseudoboletus parasiticus

The whole fungus – cap, pores and stem – is brownish yellow. The cap has a matt consistency in dry weather. The pores on the cap underside start off yellow and turn brown with age as the olive-brown spores ripen. The stem is pale brown, often curving and darker at the base. The flesh is lemon-yellow and does not change colour when cut. The taste and smell are not distinctive.

WHERE TO FIND

Parasitic on the Common Earthball (p. 156), which grows in deciduous woodland, on siliceous soil. The Parasitic Bolete usually grows in groups, more than one specimen invading the host.

FACT FILE

FAMILY **Boletaceae** SYNONYMS *Boletus parasiticus, Xerocomus parasiticus*
CAP **2–4cm** HEIGHT **3–6cm** STATUS **Widespread but uncommon**

JAN	FEB	MAR	APR	MAY	JUN	**JUL**	**AUG**	**SEP**	**OCT**	NOV	DEC

EARTHY POWDERCAP

Cystoderma amianthinum

WHERE TO FIND

In damp woods on moss and in heathland, under willows or among Bracken *Pteridium aquilinum*, especially on acid soil.

A distinctive mushroom with a saffron-coloured cap that is darker on the central umbo and a stem that has an unusual granulose or shaggy texture, making the whole mushroom completely unmistakable. The flesh is white, turning yellowish with age, and the fungus has an unpleasant, mouldy smell. The gills are crowded and the spores are white. The stem is also granulose below the ring, which may disappear altogether in older specimens.

FACT FILE

FAMILY Cystodermaceae SYNONYM Saffron Parasol CAP 2–5cm HEIGHT 2–4cm STATUS Widespread but uncommon NOTE The Earthy Powdercap may be parasitised by a violet fungus known appropriately as the Powdercap Strangler *Squamanita paradoxa*. In the invaded Earthy Powdercap, the lower part of the stem is saffron-coloured and scaly, but above this the fungus is greyish brown with no trace of granulosity

HEATH WAXCAP

Hygrocybe laeta

The waxcaps are small fungi, often brightly coloured, that grow mainly in grassland. Due to the increased use of fertiliser on grassland, however, they are becoming rarer and may eventually be classed as a protected species. The Heath Waxcap has the shiny, sticky cap that gives the waxcaps their name. The cap and stem are golden brown. The cap is striated at the edge. The greyish-white gills are decurrent, have a viscid edge and are widely spaced and uneven.

WHERE TO FIND

Grows in clumps on unimproved grassland and heaths, and even on garden lawns where no artificial fertiliser has been used.

FACT FILE

FAMILY Hygrophoraceae SYNONYM *Hygrophorus laetus* CAP 1.3–3.5cm HEIGHT 4–7cm STATUS Widespread POSSIBLE CONFUSION Some forms of the Parrot Waxcap (p. 90) are similar in colour but do not have the viscid edge to the gills

JAN	FEB	MAR	APR	MAY	JUN	JUL	**AUG**	**SEP**	**OCT**	**NOV**	DEC

SCARLET WAXCAP

Hygrocybe coccinea

The Scarlet Waxcap, as the name implies, normally has a brilliant red cap and stem, although these may fade to orange. The greasy cap is bell-shaped at first, flattening to hemispherical with age, occasionally with a central umbo. The waxy, widely spaced gills are orange-red with a yellow margin – a distinctive feature. The spores are white.

WHERE TO FIND

Grows in clumps on unimproved grassland and heaths, and even on garden lawns where no artificial fertiliser has been used.

FACT FILE

FAMILY **Hygrophoraceae** SYNONYM *Hygrophorus coccineus* CAP **2.5–5cm** HEIGHT **2.5–7cm** STATUS **Widespread** POSSIBLE CONFUSION **The Splendid Waxcap** ***Hygrocybe splendidissima*** **is similar in colour but tends to have a drier cap**

BLACKENING WAXCAP

Hygrocybe conica

The bell-shaped cap ranges in colour from yellow to orange to red but always has a central umbo. The edge of the cap is striated and uneven. As the mushroom ages, black patches appear on the cap, which eventually turns completely black. The stem is sturdy, cylindrical, usually straight though sometimes curved. It is yellow or orange, later turning black. The flesh is whitish, blackening with age. The spores are white.

Grows in closely cropped grassland in forest clearings, churchyards and gardens.

Yellow to orange cap, with darker central umbo

Whole fungus gradually blackens with age

FACT FILE

FAMILY **Hygrophoraceae** SYNONYMS *Hygrophorus nigrescens, Hygrocybe nigrescens*, **Conical Waxcap** CAP **3–5cm** HEIGHT **4–7cm** STATUS **Widespread**

BOTH SPECIES

JAN | FEB | MAR | APR | MAY | JUN | **JUL** | **AUG** | **SEP** | **OCT** | NOV | DEC

SNOWY WAXCAP

Hygrocybe virginea

Despite its name, the Snowy Waxcap is not always pure white – the cap and stem may be ochre or tinged with ochre, or have ochre or pale brownish patches. The cap is domed at first, flattening with age and often funnel-shaped when old. The flesh is white. The gills are off-white or white and run down the stem, and the spores are white. This species varies in colour and has several varieties.

WHERE TO FIND

SNOWY WAXCAP
Grows in large numbers on mossy lawns and in grassy clearings in damp woods.

PARROT WAXCAP
In grassland at high and low altitudes.

PARROT WAXCAP

Hygrocybe psittacina

Widely spaced green or orange gills

Brilliant green slimy cap, may have blue in centre

This is one of the rare green mushrooms and for that reason is easily identifiable. The glistening, slimy, bright green cap is unmistakable in the earlier stages of the fungus, but later fades to yellow. There may also be bright orange or blue patches on the cap, especially in the centre. The gills are widely spaced and yellow-green or orange, and along with the cap are slightly translucent. The thin flesh is greenish yellow. The slimy, yellow-green stem is solid at first, later hollow and paler towards the foot. The spores are white.

FACT FILE

SNOWY WAXCAP
FAMILY Hygrophoraceae SYNONYMS *Cuphophyllus virgineus*, *Hygrophorus niveus* CAP 1–4cm HEIGHT 4–7cm STATUS Widespread POSSIBLE CONFUSION Can be confused with the Ivory Woodwax (p. 91), which has a slimy cap that is inrolled at first and a scaly stem, and with the Ivory Funnel (p. 140)

PARROT WAXCAP
FAMILY Hygrophoraceae CAP 2–4cm HEIGHT 5–8cm STATUS Widespread POSSIBLE CONFUSION Heath Waxcap is similar but is never green and has a viscid edge to the gills (use a hand lens)

IVORY WOODWAX

Hygrophorus eburneus

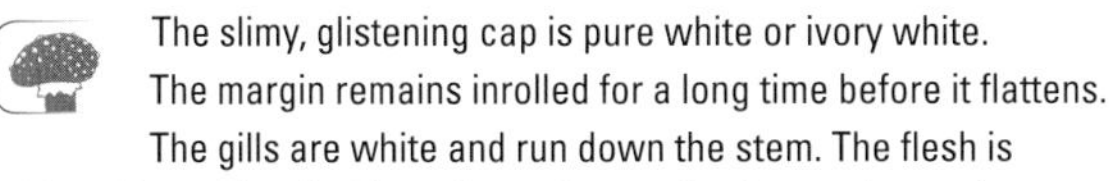

The slimy, glistening cap is pure white or ivory white. The margin remains inrolled for a long time before it flattens. The gills are white and run down the stem. The flesh is white, thin and fragile. The tall, sturdy stem is slimy and sometimes curved; it narrows at the base and is usually finely scaly at the top. The spores are white.

WHERE TO FIND

Grows under deciduous trees, mainly Beech *Fagus sylvatica*.

FACT FILE

FAMILY Hygrophoraceae CAP 4–7cm HEIGHT 7–12cm STATUS Widespread
POSSIBLE CONFUSION May be confused with 2 other white species, the Snowy Waxcap (p. 90), which has a smooth stem, and the Ivory Funnel (p. 140)

JAN FEB MAR APR MAY JUN **JUL AUG SEP OCT NOV** DEC

WOOD WOOLLYFOOT

Gymnopus peronata

WHERE TO FIND

Grows singly or in groups in deciduous and coniferous woodlands.

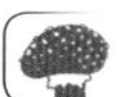

The cap is coffee-coloured to ochre, with an ochre patch in the centre, and flattens in older specimens. The edge is wrinkled and slightly wavy. The widely spaced gills are pale yellowish brown. The spores are white or cream. The thick flesh is yellowish and tastes unpleasantly peppery. The tall stem is smooth at the top, and thickly covered in white or cream hairs from the middle to the base – a very distinctive feature.

FACT FILE

FAMILY Tricholomataceae SYNONYMS *Collybia peronata, Marasmius peronatus* CAP 3–6cm HEIGHT 7–9cm STATUS Widespread and common POSSIBLE CONFUSION May be mistaken for The Deceiver (p. 41)

BOTH SPECIES

JAN | FEB | MAR | APR | MAY | JUN | **JUL** | **AUG** | **SEP** | **OCT** | **NOV** | DEC

SPOTTED TOUGHSHANK

Collybia maculata

The cap is white, splashed with reddish-brown patches. The edge is paler and becomes upturned in older specimens, but is inrolled when the fungus is young. The crowded gills are white. The spores are white or cream. The thin flesh is white and tastes bitter. The stem is smooth and white at the top, and stained with brown towards the base.

Smooth stem, white at the top, stained brown at the bottom

White cap spotted with reddish-brown patches

WHERE TO FIND

SPOTTED TOUGHSHANK
Grows in large or small groups under conifers.

BUTTER CAP
Grows in groups on pine needles and leaves. It prefers a rich, neutral soil.

Cap greyish-brown, darker at the margin, greasy texture

BUTTER CAP

Collybia butyracea

The greyish-brown cap is umbonate at first, always remaining hemispherical but darkening at the margin. It has a greasy or buttery texture – hence the species' common name – and turns paler in dry weather. The white or cream-coloured gills are crowded. The grey-brown flesh has a watery consistency. The stem is straight and reddish brown, paler towards the top, and sometimes covered in fluffy white mycelium at the base.

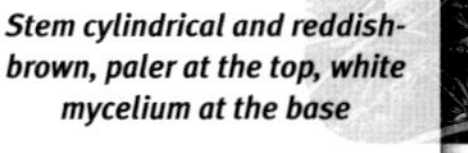

Stem cylindrical and reddish-brown, paler at the top, white mycelium at the base

FACT FILE

SPOTTED TOUGHSHANK
FAMILY **Tricholomataceae**
SYNONYM *Rhodocollybia maculata*
CAP **6–10cm** HEIGHT **7–10cm**
STATUS **Widespread and common**

BUTTER CAP
FAMILY **Tricholomataceae**
SYNONYM *Rhodocollybia butyracea*
CAP **3–7cm** HEIGHT **6–9cm**
STATUS **Widespread and common**

JAN FEB MAR **APR** **MAY** **JUN** JUL AUG SEP OCT NOV DEC

PINECONE CAP

Strobilurus tenacellus

WHERE TO FIND

On pine or, rarely, spruce cones, sometimes on the individual scales. Found only in spring, so look for it then.

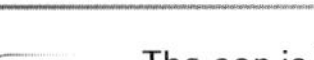

The cap is hemispherical, flattening with age. It is tobacco-brown, slightly paler in the centre. The stem, which is sometimes curved to allow efficient spore release, is brownish yellow but usually distinctly paler at the top. The gills are white, as are the spores. The flesh is off-white and thin, and has a bitter taste.

FACT FILE

FAMILY Physalacriaceae CAP 1-2.5cm HEIGHT 4–7cm STATUS Widespread

POSSIBLE CONFUSION The Conifercone Cap (p. 95) is similar but is an autumn species

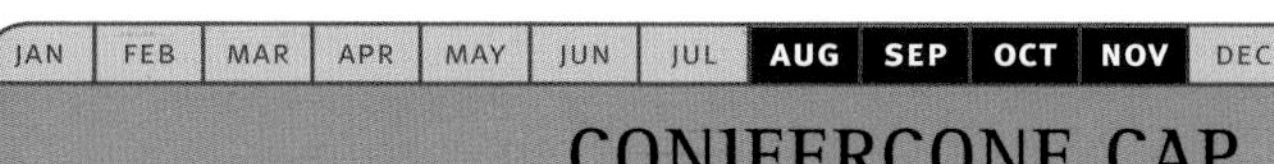

CONIFERCONE CAP

Baeospora myosura

The ochre to date-brown cap is hemispherical, flattening with age but sometimes leaving a small central umbo. The gills are white to pale grey and very crowded. The stem is the width and colour of a mouse's tail, hence the alternative common name for the fungus. It tapers into a root-like structure that is covered in stiff hairs. The flesh is pale brown and thin.

WHERE TO FIND

Grows exclusively on cones of coniferous trees, sometimes on the individual scales.

FACT FILE

FAMILY Marasmiaceae SYNONYM Mousetail Collybia CAP <2cm HEIGHT 2–6cm STATUS Widespread POSSIBLE CONFUSION May be confused with Pinecone Cap (p. 94), but that is a spring species

JAN | FEB | MAR | APR | MAY | JUN | **JUL** | **AUG** | **SEP** | **OCT** | **NOV** | DEC

BLOODRED WEBCAP

Cortinarius sanguineus

WHERE TO FIND

Grows in groups in deciduous, coniferous and mixed woods, but usually under conifers.

This species is entirely blood-red, including the flesh. The cap is hemispherical at first, flattening with age and the edge becoming torn in places. It is covered in fibrils when young, becoming downy as it matures. The tall, thin, fibrous stem is covered in pale yellow or pink down when young. The spores are rusty brown.

FACT FILE

FAMILY Cortinariaceae SYNONYMS *C. puniceus*, *Dermocybe sanguinea* CAP 3–5cm HEIGHT 4–7cm STATUS Widespread but uncommon POSSIBLE CONFUSION In the similar Surprise Webcap *C. semisanguineus*, only the gills are blood-red – the cap and stem are yellow

JAN FEB MAR APR MAY JUN **JUL AUG SEP OCT NOV DEC**

SCURFY TWIGLET

Tubaria furfuracea

The cap is cinnamon-brown, becoming paler and slightly scurfy in dry weather. The margin bears the remnants of a white veil that is shown as tiny flakes. The gills are brown and may run down the stem a little way. The spores are yellow-brown. The stem is tall and slender. It can be the same colour as the cap or darker brown, and is surrounded at the base by a fluffy white mycelium. The pale brown flesh is thin. Found growing in groups or small clusters.

WHERE TO FIND

On the ground in woods and grassland, on all types of dead or decaying wood from deciduous trees, including wood chips and sawdust.

FACT FILE

FAMILY Inocybaceae CAP 1-4cm HEIGHT 1–4cm STATUS Widespread and common POSSIBLE CONFUSION May be confused with the many other small brown-capped species, but especially *T. hiemalis*

JAN	FEB	MAR	**APR**	**MAY**	**JUN**	**JUL**	**AUG**	**SEP**	**OCT**	NOV	DEC

YELLOW FIELDCAP

Bolbitius titubans

The fresh, slimy, bright yellow cap is distinctive. It is ovoid at first, expanding to become shallowly hemispherical as it ages, and at this time becomes furrowed and faded. The crowded gills are off-white or beige, darkening with age as the brown spores mature. The tall white stem is long and thin. There is no ring.

WHERE TO FIND

Grows individually or in groups on rotting straw, compost and well-manured grass. Very fleeting, lasting only 24 hours.

FACT FILE

FAMILY **Bolbitiaceae** SYNONYMS *B. vitellinus, B. fragilis*
CAP **2–5cm** HEIGHT **4–8cm** STATUS **Widespread and common**

RICKEN'S CONECAP

Conocybe rickenii

The cap is orange brown drying cream, sometimes with whitish fibrils at the edge. It is conical to bell-shaped, barely expanding even when mature. The gills are cream to start with then orange brown, and they are crowded. The spores are brown. The flesh is grey-brown under the cap, brownish in the stem. The long stem is cylindrical and quite slender, thickening slightly towards the base. It is whitish to start with, turning brown with age and has no ring.

WHERE TO FIND

On dung and nitrate-rich soil.

FACT FILE

FAMILY Bolbitiaceae CAP 1-5cm HEIGHT 4–8cm STATUS Widespread and common

JAN FEB MAR APR MAY JUN JUL **AUG SEP OCT NOV DEC**

STICKY SCALYCAP

Pholiota gummosa

WHERE TO FIND

Grows in dense clumps on decayed wood, usually on the ground and then always from partially buried wood.

The yellowish-white cap, which is often slightly green tinged, is egg-shaped at first, flattening to hemispherical with a ragged margin. It is sticky when damp, and is covered in small brown scales that are widely spaced apart. The flesh is yellow or cream-coloured. The gills are yellow, turning rust-coloured as the purple-brown spores ripen. The long, scaly white stem has a faint ring two-thirds of the way up and is often curved to ensure the cap is parallel to the ground for spore dispersal.

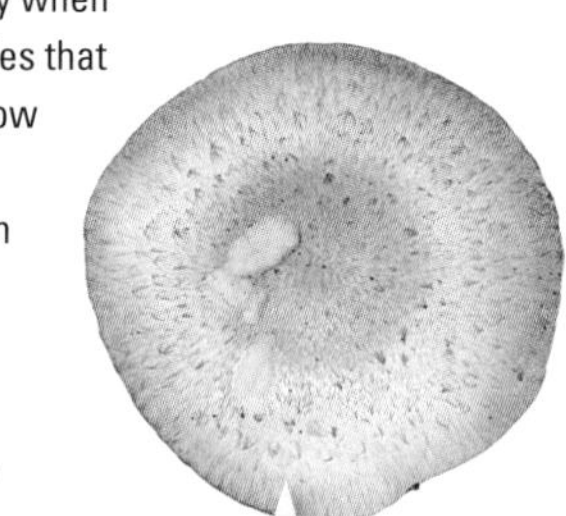

Yellowish-white cap, sometimes green-tinged

Grows in large clumps

FACT FILE

FAMILY Strophariaceae CAP 3–6cm HEIGHT 6–10cm STATUS Widespread
POSSIBLE CONFUSION The poisonous Shaggy Scalycap (p. 153) is similar but its scales are much darker, denser and shaggier

DUNG ROUNDHEAD

Stropharia semiglobata

The pale yellow-brown to straw-coloured cap is hemispherical at first, widening but never completely flattening. It is smooth when dry and sticky when wet. The flesh is thin and white. The dark brown gills are broad and triangular. The tall stem is the same colour as the cap and straight. The dark ring, which is quite low on the stem, may be almost invisible and disappear entirely in older specimens.

On dung of herbivores.

FACT FILE

FAMILY Strophariaceae CAP 2–4cm HEIGHT 5–9cm STATUS Widespread and common POSSIBLE CONFUSION The similar Egghead Mottlegill *Panaeolus semiovatus* has an ovoid or egg-shaped cap

JAN | FEB | MAR | **APR** | **MAY** | **JUN** | **JUL** | **AUG** | **SEP** | **OCT** | **NOV** | DEC

FIRERUG INKCAP

Coprinellus domesticus

The egg-shaped cap is light brown and densely covered in tiny cream flakes, which are the remnants of a veil. The margin becomes ragged in older specimens as it starts to deliquesce. The crowded gills are white when young, turning brown as the black spores mature. The thin brown flesh has no taste or smell. The white stem is thicker than in most species in the genus and has no ring. The most distinctive feature is the thick mesh of orange mycelium at the base of the stem, known as an ozonium, which spreads around the fungus (hence its common name) but is not always present.

WHERE TO FIND

Grows on dead and decaying wood of deciduous trees including buried wood; also found indoors (hence its scientific name), growing on rafters and waterlogged carpets.

FACT FILE

FAMILY **Psathyrellaceae** SYNONYM *Coprinus domesticus* CAP **3–7cm** HEIGHT **6–9cm** STATUS **Widespread but uncommon** POSSIBLE CONFUSION **May be confused with the Glistening Inkcap** **(p. 58)**

FAIRY INKCAP

Coprinellus disseminatus

The pleated cap of this tiny fungus is ovoid at first, expanding to bell-shaped, each furrow in it corresponding to a single gill. It has a woolly mouse-grey surface with a central brownish centre. The brown flesh is so thin that it is almost invisible. The gills are white then grey and eventually blackening. Unlike some other inkcaps, the Fairy Inkcap does not deliquesce and has quite a long lifespan despite its fragility.

WHERE TO FIND

On dead wood of deciduous trees. Easy to find and unmistakable, as it always grows in huge numbers.

Pleated, egg-shaped cap

Grows in huge masses

FACT FILE

FAMILY Psathyrellaceae
SYNONYMS *Coprinus disseminatus*, Fairy's Bonnet CAP <1cm
HEIGHT 2–5cm
STATUS Widespread and common

JAN | FEB | MAR | APR | MAY | JUN | **JUL** | **AUG** | **SEP** | **OCT** | **NOV** | DEC

GIANT CLUB

Clavariadelphus pistillaris

WHERE TO FIND

Under deciduous trees, mostly Beech *Fagus sylvatica* on calcareous soils.

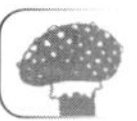

This fungus is the shape of a wooden club and might be a deadly weapon if it were the right size! It varies in colour from orange to ochre, and may even be bright yellow. The club fungi or fairy clubs are related to the coral fungi. The spores are released from the top of the 'club'.

FACT FILE

FAMILY Clavariadelphaceae HEIGHT 8–20cm WIDTH 2–6cm STATUS Widespread but uncommon POSSIBLE CONFUSION The Club Coral Fungus *C. truncatus* looks similar, but as if its top has been sliced off. This edible species is bright yellow and grows under conifers on limestone soil

UPRIGHT CORAL

Ramaria stricta

The coral fungi are usually very small and resemble small branching corals in the sea. The Upright Coral has tightly packed parallel branches that grow from short trunks. The colour ranges from cinnamon to pale ochre, with yellowish tips. The spores are white and the fungus bruises dark red when damaged or cut.

WHERE TO FIND

One of the few coral fungi that grows on wood, favouring rotting wood in mixed woodlands.

FACT FILE

FAMILY Gomphaceae HEIGHT 3-10cm WIDTH 3-8cm STATUS Widespread but uncommon POSSIBLE CONFUSION Other species of coral fungi

JAN FEB MAR APR **MAY JUN JUL AUG SEP** OCT NOV DEC

STINKHORN

Phallus impudicus

WHERE TO FIND

Grows in humus in deciduous woods.

This is another distinctive fungus. It grows from an off-white 'egg', which when cut open reveals a greenish jelly surrounding what will eventually become the cap. The remains of the 'egg' remain attached to the body of the fungus as the white stem shoots upwards. The stem is pitted and hollow, and the cap is covered in an olive-green slime that contains the spores and emits an appalling odour. This attracts flies, which then carry the spores away to disperse them.

Greenish slime on top attracts flies

White hollow 'stem' growing out of 'egg'

FACT FILE

FAMILY Phallaceae
CAP 1–3cm HEIGHT 15–20cm
STATUS Widespread and common
POSSIBLE CONFUSION The Dog Stinkhorn *Mutinus caninus* has a similar shape, but is smaller and the stem is pale orange; it grows on rotting humus in forests

YELLOW STAGSHORN

Calocera viscosa

The stagshorns are miniature versions of the coral fungi but their flesh has a jelly-like consistency. The Yellow Stagshorn is bright yellow all over except for the tips of the branches, which are sometimes orange. The flesh is soft and elastic. The white spores are carried on the tips of the branches. Its gelatinous texture makes the fungus hard to pick, especially if it is deeply embedded.

WHERE TO FIND

Grows on the rotten wood of dead conifers.

FACT FILE

FAMILY Dacrymycetacae HEIGHT 3–8cm STATUS Widespread but uncommon
POSSIBLE CONFUSION The Yellow Fairy Club *Clavulinopsis laeticolor* is similar, but is not branched

JAN	FEB	MAR	APR	MAY	JUN	**JUL**	**AUG**	**SEP**	**OCT**	**NOV**	DEC

SPLITGILL

Schizophyllum commune

WHERE TO FIND

Grows in tufts or groups on all types of wood, on ferns and even on straw. Look for it after rain, when it fruits.

The leathery fan-shaped brackets are often lobed or fused together at the base. The upper surface is densely covered in erect grey-brown hairs, which are paler when the fungus is dry. The undersurface consists of radiating gills that are split lengthwise. The spores are white. The tough grey-brown flesh is thin. The stem is eccentric or missing.

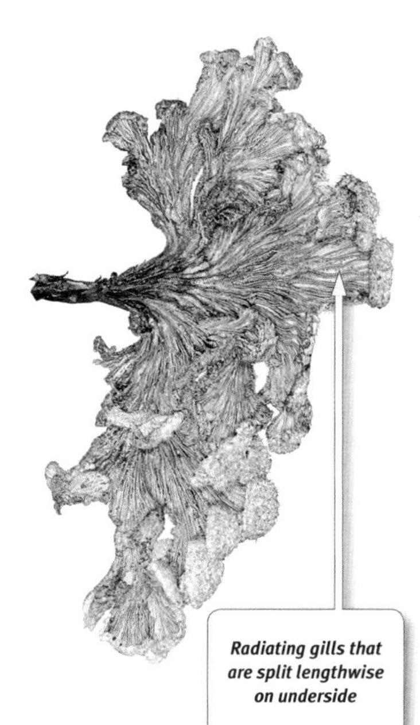

Radiating gills that are split lengthwise on underside

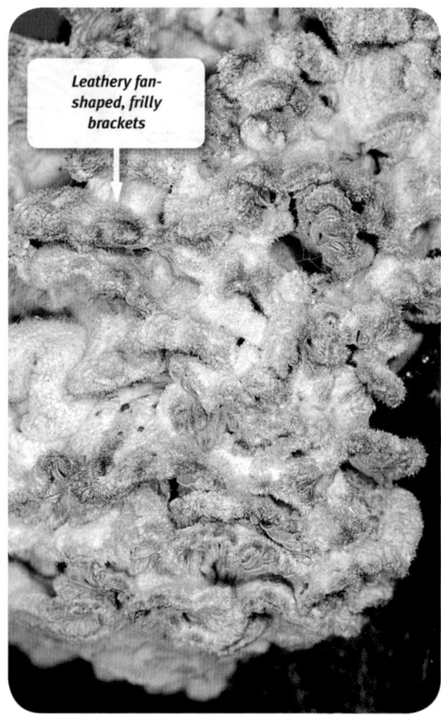

Leathery fan-shaped, frilly brackets

FACT FILE

FAMILY Schyzophyllaceae SYNONYM Common Porecrust BRACKET 1–3.5cm THICKNESS 1-3mm STATUS Widespread and common NOTE Said to be the most widespread fungus in the world – it is found on every continent except Antarctica

PEELING OYSTERLING

Crepidotus mollis

The plain or scaly cap is fan- or kidney-shaped and whitish or beige, turning darker in wet weather. The surface is covered with a detachable gelatinous layer in young specimens, but this may wash away in heavy rain. The undersurface consists of crowded white gills that become pale brown with age and radiate from the point where the cap is attached to the tree. There is no stem. The spores are brown. The tough grey-brown flesh is thin.

WHERE TO FIND

Grows in tufts or groups on all types of dead or decaying wood from deciduous trees.

FACT FILE

FAMILY **Crepidotaceae** CAP **2–7cm** HEIGHT **0.5–1cm** STATUS **Widespread and common**
POSSIBLE CONFUSION **The Variable Oysterling *C. variabilis* is similar, but is smaller and does not have a detachable gelatinous layer on the cap surface**

JAN FEB MAR APR MAY JUN **JUL AUG SEP OCT** NOV DEC

COPPER SPIKE

Chroogomphus rutilus

WHERE TO FIND

Grows singly or in small groups, under pine trees and, rarely, other conifers.

The greasy cap is a glistening coppery colour. It is convex at first, becoming slightly flatter later with a small umbo, and the edge remains inrolled for a long time. It barely covers the widely spaced reddish-ochre gills, which run down the stem. The flesh is orange-red, tending to darken when cut or bruised. The stem is reddish near the top, yellower below, covered in small red scales, narrowing towards the top and sometimes swollen in the centre.

FACT FILE

FAMILY Gomphidiaceae SYNONYM *Gomphidius viscidus* CAP 5–10cm
HEIGHT 6–13cm STATUS Widespread but uncommon

JAN FEB MAR APR MAY JUN JUL AUG SEP OCT NOV DEC

WINTER POLYPORE

Polyporus brumalis

This polypore has a relatively tall, thin stem, making it look like a bolete. The smooth cap is round with a slightly inrolled edge and is greyish brown in colour. The pores on the underside are white and large, expanding with age. The spores are white. The stem is slender and tapering, and is off-white in colour.

WHERE TO FIND

Found on the rotting wood of a number of deciduous trees especially birches.

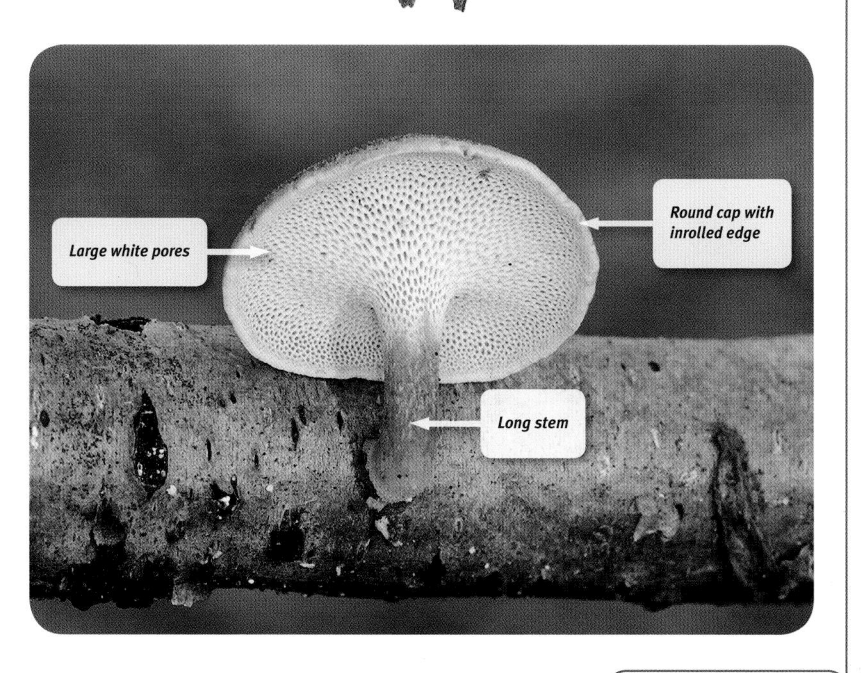

FACT FILE

FAMILY Polyporaceae CAP 4–8cm HEIGHT 4–5cm STATUS Widespread but uncommon POSSIBLE CONFUSION Fringed Polypore (p. 112) is similar but its stem is covered in brown scales and its pores are much smaller

JAN FEB **MAR APR MAY JUN JUL AUG SEP OCT NOV DEC**

FRINGED POLYPORE

Polyporus ciliatus

WHERE TO FIND

Found on the rotting wood (usually logs and fallen branches) of a number of deciduous trees.

This is another polypore with a distinct thin central stem covered in bands of brown scales. The cap is round, often with a central depression, is greyish brown and is covered in small bristles, especially at the edge, hence the species' name. The pores are white to cream, turning brownish with age. The flesh is white.

FACT FILE

FAMILY Polyporaceae CAP 4–8cm HEIGHT 4–5cm STATUS Widespread but uncommon
POSSIBLE CONFUSION May be mistaken for Winter Polypore (p. 111), but the stem of that species lacks scales and its pores are larger

JAN | FEB | MAR | APR | MAY | JUN | JUL | AUG | SEP | OCT | NOV | DEC

COMMON MAZEGILL

Datronia mollis

The upper surface of this thin, tough leathery, mainly resupinate, bracket is velvety, brown initially and then turning black, and its undersurface is white discolouring brown with age and bruising. The flesh is pale brown. The pore surface is covered with a grey to white bloom that disappears if the fungus is handled.

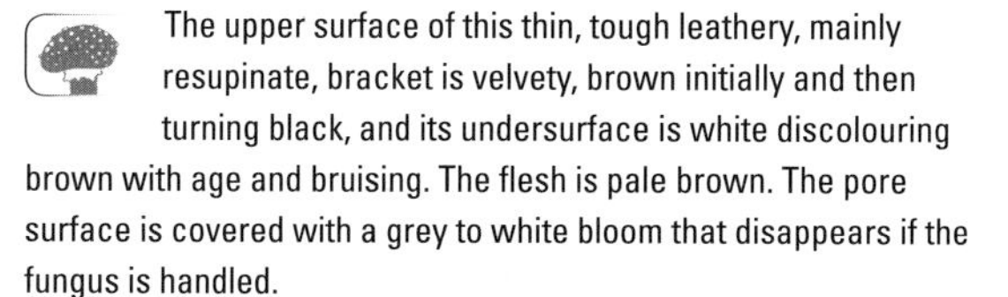

WHERE TO FIND

On dead deciduous wood.

FACT FILE

FAMILY Polyporaceae SYNONYM *Trametes mollis* CAP 1–7cm STATUS Widespread and common POSSIBLE CONFUSION The related Oak Mazegill *Daedala quercina* is similar but has pale ochre brackets; it attacks oak. The Benzoin Bracket (p. 74) is also similar but restricted to conifers

JAN | FEB | MAR | APR | MAY | JUN | JUL | AUG | SEP | OCT | NOV | DEC

HOOF FUNGUS

Fomes fomentarius

WHERE TO FIND

Parasitic on deciduous trees, mainly birches, Beech *Fagus sylvatica* and Sycamore *Acer pseudoplatanus.*

This thick, lumpy bracket is the colour and shape of a horse's hoof, hence its common name. The upper surface is ridged and banded with various shades of grey and brown, the ridges a consequence of year on year growth. The underside is whitish, ageing brownish, darkening when bruised.

FACT FILE

FAMILY Polyporaceae SYNONYMS Tinder Bracket, *Polyporus fomentarius* DIAMETER 10–50cm HEIGHT 3–25cm STATUS Widespread and common NOTE The alternative common name stems from the fact that the fungus used to be placed in tinderboxes for striking friction matches; it is still useful for lighting a fire in the wild owing to its slow-burning property. It is also useful as a styptic

JAN | FEB | MAR | APR | MAY | JUN | JUL | AUG | SEP | OCT | NOV | DEC

PURPLEPORE BRACKET

Trichaptum abietinum

The fruiting body initially covers the tree in a crust but eventually forms semicircular, kidney- or hoof-shaped brackets that are attached directly without a stem. The irregular upper surface of the thin bracket is felty and banded with concentric rings of grey or brown. In damp places, the brackets may be covered with green algae. The underside is violet, with irregular pores that tear into coarse, pointed excrescences.

WHERE TO FIND

Grows in large numbers, sometimes in their hundreds, on dead conifers.

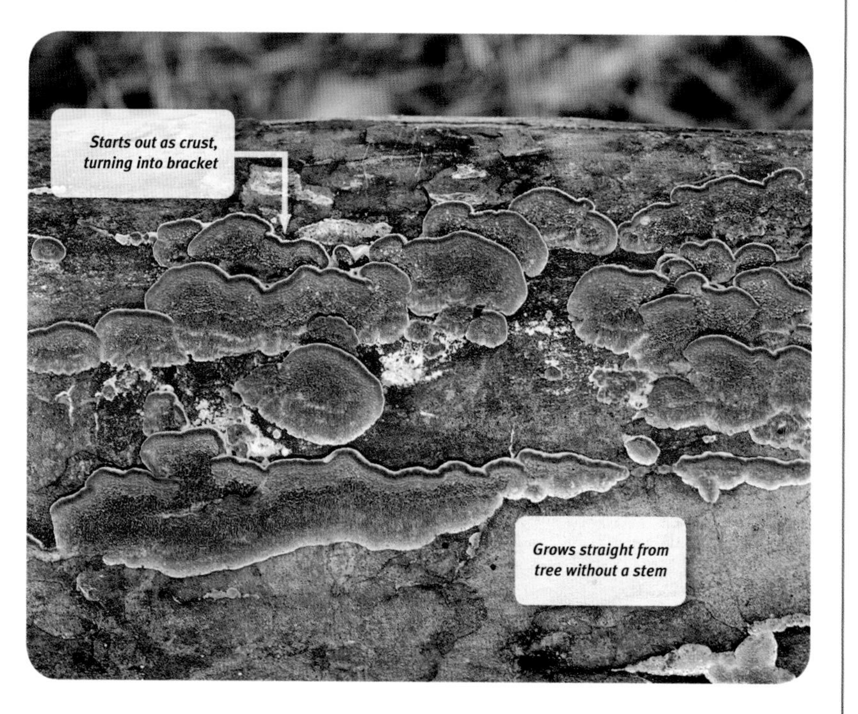

FACT FILE

FAMILY Polyporaceae SYNONYM *Coriolus abietinus* DIAMETER 1-3cm THICKNESS 1–3cm STATUS Widespread but uncommon POSSIBLE CONFUSION The Silverleaf Fungus *Chondrostereum purpureum* is similar, but is thicker and almost confined to deciduous trees

LUMPY BRACKET

Trametes gibbosa

WHERE TO FIND

Parasitic on deciduous trees, especially Beech *Fagus sylvatica*; very occasionally found on conifers.

The fruiting body is semicircular or hoof-shaped, with off-white upper and lower surfaces. The irregular upper surface of the bracket is felty, and in damp places may be covered with green algae. The flesh is white, and the pores are elongated.

FACT FILE

FAMILY Polyporaceae CAP 5–20cm THICKNESS 3–5cm STATUS Widespread and common POSSIBLE CONFUSION The Oak Mazegill *Daedala quercina* is similar, but its upper surface is varied shades of ochre

JAN | FEB | MAR | APR | MAY | JUN | JUL | AUG | SEP | OCT | NOV | DEC

HAIRY CURTAIN CRUST

Stereum hirsutum

The curtain crusts are, as the name implies, fungi that form a crust over the wood on which they grow. The crust then develops into superimposed caps that are welded together to form large masses. In the Hairy Curtain Crust, the upper surface is velvety and even hairy, with concentric rings in various shades of yellow, white and brown, the colour being darker where the cap is attached to the wood. The underside is smooth, orange-yellow at first and then ochre, and contains tiny pores. The edge of the cap is undulating and lobed, and is bright yellow in young specimens. The flesh and spores are white.

WHERE TO FIND

Found on all types of rotting timber and stumps from deciduous trees, and on new tree growth in autumn.

FACT FILE

FAMILY **Stereaceae** CAP **1-3cm** STATUS **Widespread and common**

JAN | FEB | MAR | APR | MAY | JUN | JUL | AUG | SEP | OCT | NOV | DEC

BLEEDING BROADLEAF CRUST

Stereum rugosum

WHERE TO FIND

On stumps, logs and fallen branches of deciduous wood, especially Hazel *Corylus avellana*.

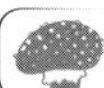

This curtain crust is one of a group that 'bleed' red droplets when cut or damaged. It only occasionally develops into a series of caps or brackets. The upper surface is a uniform greyish ochre, often cracking when dry. The thin flesh and spores are white. The congealed 'blood' can collect in strips on the surface of the fungus as it ages.

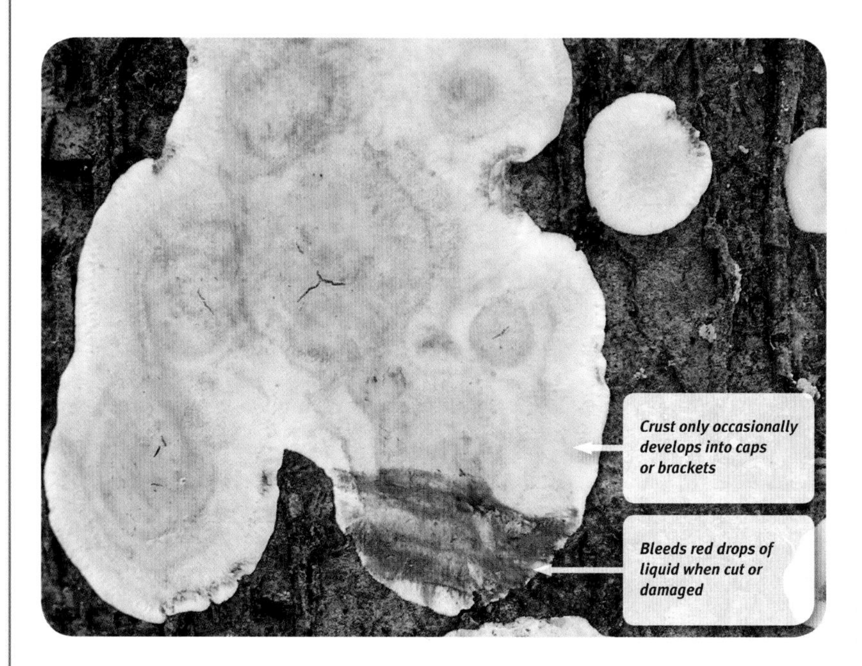

FACT FILE

FAMILY Stereaceae CAP 2–5cm STATUS Widespread and common POSSIBLE CONFUSION The Bleeding Conifer Crust *S. sanguinolentum* looks similar but is paler with white edges; it is found only on conifers. The Bleeding Oak Crust *S. gausapatum* is also similar but found only on oaks. Both of these species turn brown or exude a red or brown liquid when cut or bruised

JAN | FEB | MAR | APR | MAY | JUN | JUL | AUG | SEP | OCT | NOV | DEC

YELLOWING CURTAIN CRUST

Stereum subtomentosum

INDIVIDUAL SPECIMEN

Fan-shaped brackets with pale edge and dark centre

This curtain crust is pale yellow with concentric greyish-orange to greyish-white zones. There is no stem. If the surface is scratched it will turn yellow, hence the species' common name. The underside is greyish white to ochre and smooth, the pores being invisible to the naked eye. The spores are white.

WHERE TO FIND

On rotting timber and stumps in deciduous woods, mostly Beech *Fagus sylvatica.*

FACT FILE

FAMILY Stereaceae SYNONYM Yellow Curtain Crust CAP 2–8cm STATUS Widespread but uncommon POSSIBLE CONFUSION In the similar *S. insignitum* the upper surface has concentric bands of darker and paler reddish-brown and a bright yellow edge. The Turkeytail *Trametes versicolor* is also similar but darker and with more marked concentric rings that are greyer; it is much more common than Yellowing Curtain Crust

Surface turns yellow when damaged

JAN FEB MAR APR **MAY JUN JUL AUG SEP** OCT NOV DEC

DYER'S MAZEGILL

Phaeolus schweinitzii

WHERE TO FIND

On trunks and roots of dead and dying conifers.

The brackets are deep yellow and irregular in shape when young, becoming more circular or kidney-shaped and turning rust-brown with a yellow edge. The velvety upper surface is cracked and pitted. The spongy yellow flesh later turns brown. The tubes on the yellow-brown underside of the cap end in wide, elongated pores.

FACT FILE

FAMILY Fomitopsidaceae SYNONYM *Polyporus schweinitzii* DIAMETER 10–30cm THICKNESS 0.5–2cm STATUS Widespread and common NOTE Traditionally used to make a dye in N Europe, hence its common name

JAN | FEB | MAR | APR | MAY | JUN | JUL | AUG | SEP | OCT | NOV | DEC

BIRCH POLYPORE

Piptoporus betulinus

The thick bracket is rounded at first, expanding into a fan- or hoof-shaped fungus. The upper surface is greyish brown to brown, thin and dry, and it chips away in patches. The margin is whitish, sometimes with a raised rim that covers the pores at the edge of the white underside. The crowded tubes end in small round pores. The stem, if any, is short and lateral. The flesh is elastic at first, becoming corky in mature specimens.

WHERE TO FIND

Exclusively attacks birches, causing white rot.

FACT FILE

FAMILY Fomitopsidaceae
SYNONYM Razorstrop Fungus, *Polyporus betulinus*
DIAMETER 10–20cm
THICKNESS 2–6cm
STATUS Widespread and common
NOTE The brackets were once cut up and used to sharpen cut-throat razors, hence its alternative common name. They also have styptic properties

JAN | FEB | MAR | APR | MAY | JUN | JUL | AUG | SEP | OCT | NOV | DEC

RED-BELTED POLYPORE

Fomitopsis pinicola

WHERE TO FIND

Parasitic on pine trees.

The thick bracket is rounded at first, expanding into a fan- or hoof-shaped fungus. The upper surface is blackish to brownish and contains so much resin that it will melt if a flame is applied to it. The margin is paler, sometimes red, but despite the species' common name it can be yellow, orange or white. The underside is pale yellow and sometimes drips with a whitish latex.

FACT FILE

FAMILY Fomitopsidaceae
SYNONYM *Ungulina marginata*
DIAMETER 10–25cm HEIGHT 3–10cm
STATUS Widespread and common
POSSIBLE CONFUSION The Rosy Cork *F. rosea* is similar but the whole bracket is tinged with pink and it doesn't produce resin. It is also parasitic on conifers, but occurs only at high altitude

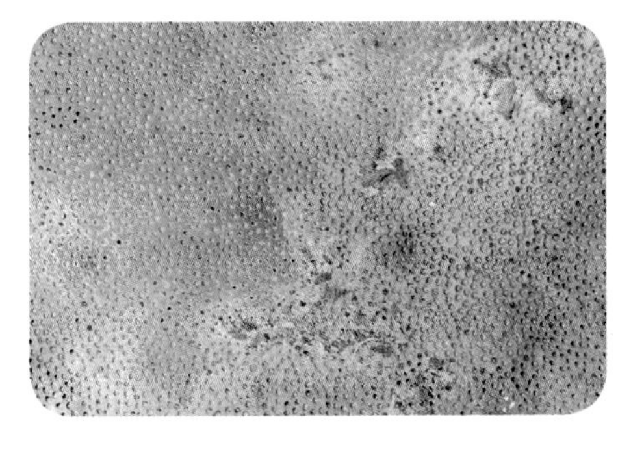

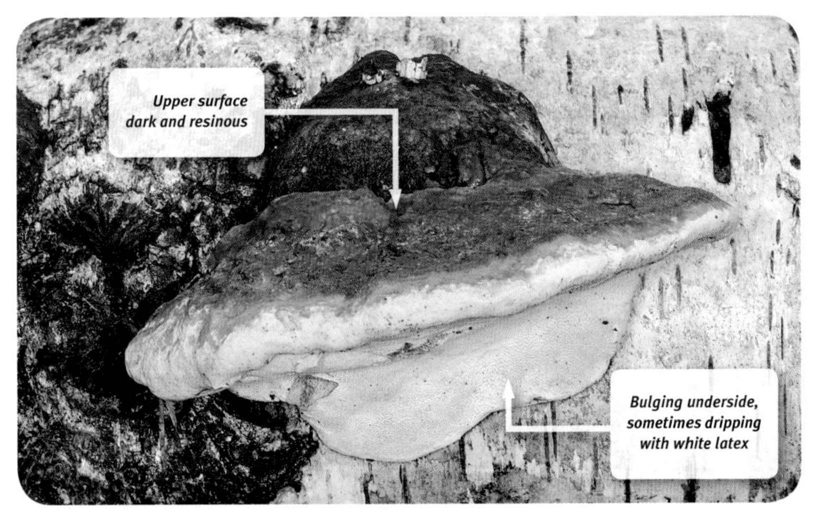

TOP: *PORES.*

JAN | FEB | MAR | APR | MAY | JUN | **JUL** | **AUG** | **SEP** | **OCT** | NOV | DEC

HETEROMORPHIC POLYPORE

Antrodia heteromorpha

This fungus initially forms a crust, which then develops into stemless brackets and nodules covering a large area of tree stumps and standing trunks. The upper surface is white or cream and may be smooth or covered in silky fibrils. The underside is also white and contains small pores. Caps and crust exist simultaneously on the tree. As the species' name implies, the shape is very changeable, but the large area covered on the tree, the different shapes of crust and brackets, and the pure white colour makes it easy to identify to genus, but there are other very similar species of *Antrodia*.

WHERE TO FIND

Almost always in large numbers on conifers, especially spruces and more rarely on pines, in which it causes a brown rot.

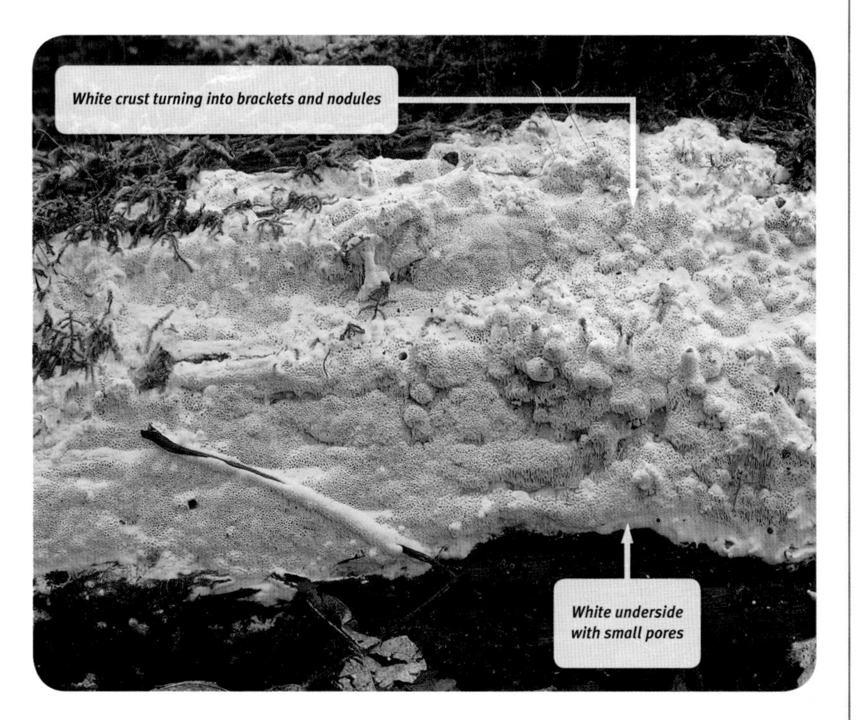

FACT FILE

FAMILY Fomitopsidaceae DIAMETER 3–10cm STATUS Widespread and common

JAN | FEB | MAR | APR | MAY | JUN | JUL | AUG | SEP | OCT | NOV | DEC

ROOT ROT

Heterobasidion annosum

The upper surface of the large, tough single bracket has rusty-red concentric rings, paling to yellow and with a white edge. The underside is white, with small, crowded tubes that end in pores. The spores are also white. When the weather is humid, the fungus produces asexual spores, known as conidiophores, which can live in the soil for 10 months; this stage has the separate scientific name *Spiniger meineckellus*.

WHERE TO FIND

A dangerous parasite that destroys conifers, more rarely found on hardwoods; usually grows near the base of the host's trunk.

FACT FILE

FAMILY Bondarzewiaceae SYNONYM *Fomes annosus*
CAP 1–40cm STATUS Widespread and common

SMOKY BRACKET

Bjerkandera adusta

The individual brackets are small and greyish white, becoming almost black, growing in large, dense, superimposed clumps. They have a white margin and are shallow and fan-shaped at first, later becoming kidney-shaped. The underside is covered in tiny pores, and is light grey darkening to cinder-grey with age, giving the fungus the appearance of having been damaged by smoke. The flesh is white, tough and leathery.

WHERE TO FIND

On dead wood, especially Beech *Fagus sylvatica*, often in huge groups.

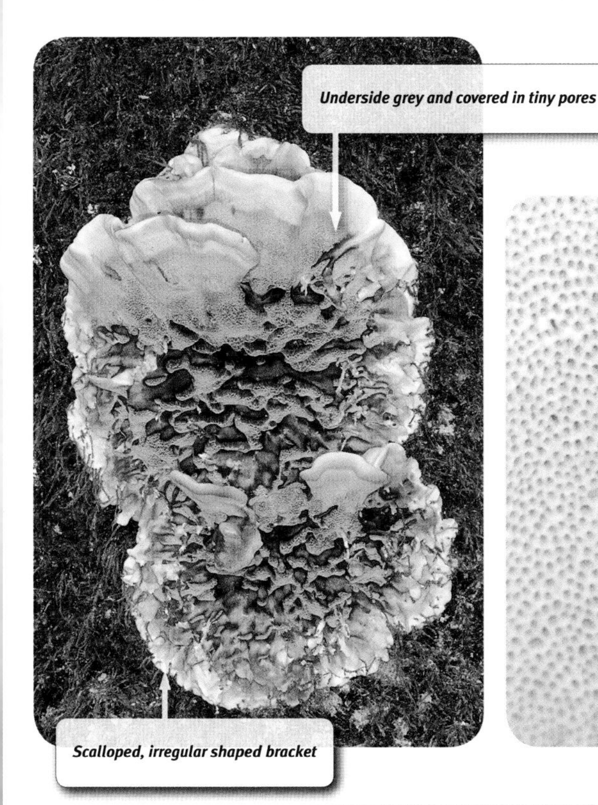

FACT FILE

FAMILY Meruliaceae SYNONYMS Burnt Polypore, *Leptoporus adustus* DIAMETER 2–4cm STATUS Widespread and common POSSIBLE CONFUSION The Big Smoky Bracket *B. fumosa* is similar but produces larger brackets with a cream underside and smells of aniseed when fresh

JAN | FEB | MAR | APR | MAY | JUN | JUL | AUG | SEP | OCT | NOV | DEC

ARTIST'S BRACKET

Ganoderma applanatum

The scalloped, irregular bracket can grow to an enormous size. The upper surface is ochre, covered in concentric furrows. The underside is whitish, then brownish black, often with a dusting of the chocolate-brown spores. The flesh is white, tough and leathery. The underside is sometimes covered in nipple-like galls produced by the fly *Agathomya wankowiczi*.

WHERE TO FIND

Grows on dead branches, trunks and stumps of deciduous trees, or very occasionally on conifers.

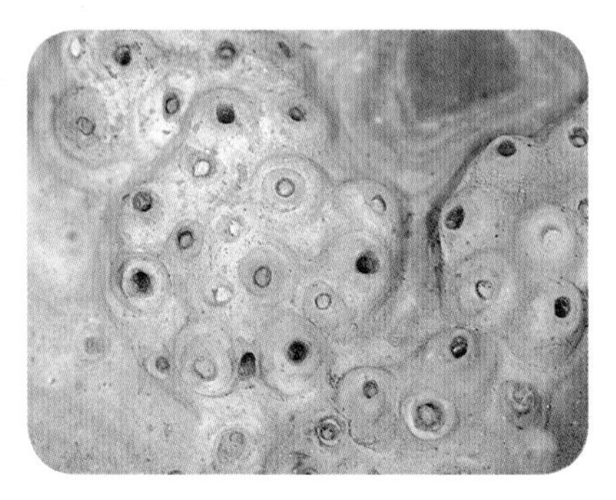

RIGHT: *UNDERSIDE COVERED IN GALLS.*

FACT FILE

FAMILY Ganodermataceae CAP <70cm THICKNESS 10–15cm STATUS Widespread and uncommon NOTE The origin of the species' common name is that when the underside is white it can be used for drawing pictures, as it turns darker when pressure is applied

Upperside hard and concentrically furrowed

Found only on beech

COLLARED EARTHSTAR

Geastrum triplex

The earthstars have an extremely unusual shape, with a central globular sac, like a tiny football, containing the spores and surrounded by a protective layer that splits open into a star shape and bends underneath the sac when the fungus is mature. The points of the star often crack in dry weather. When the sac is revealed, a hole forms at the top, from which the dark spores are emitted in smoke-like swirls when the fragile ball is hit by a raindrop. The stalk is absent or very short. The whole fungus is light brown. The Collared Earthstar has an extra fleshy layer (the collar) between the rays of the star and the ball that is lacking in other earthstars.

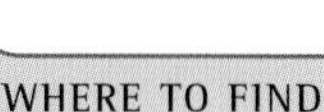

Found in shady places in humus and leaf litter mainly under deciduous trees in thick woods.

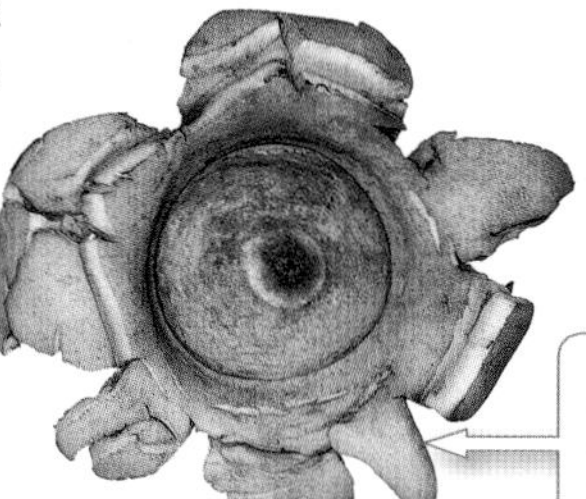

CLOSE-UP SHOWING COLLAR.

Points of star cracking in dry weather

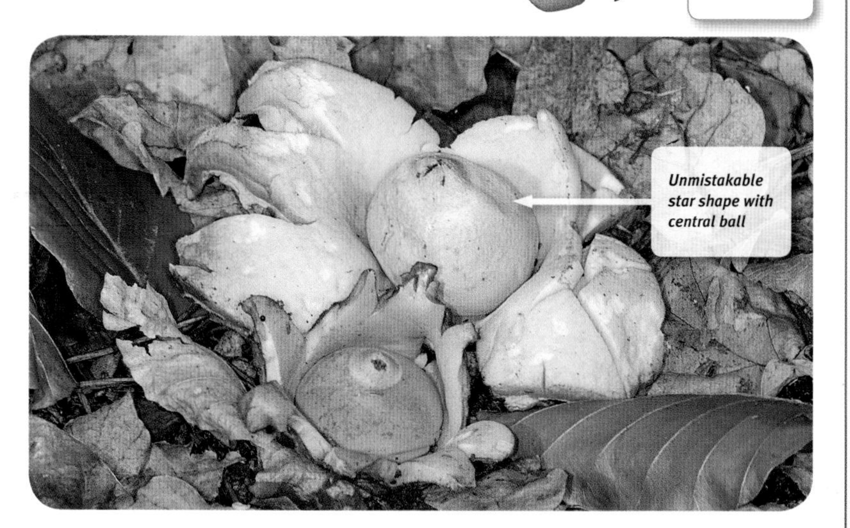

Unmistakable star shape with central ball

FACT FILE

FAMILY **Geastraceae** FRUITING BODY DIAMETER **5–10cm** STATUS **Widespread and common**
POSSIBLE CONFUSION **The Sessile Earthstar *G. sessile* is similar, but smaller and lacks a fleshy collar**

JAN FEB MAR APR MAY JUN **JUL AUG SEP OCT NOV** DEC

TIGER'S EYE

Coltricia perennis

WHERE TO FIND

On sandy, acid soils in woodland and on heaths.

This is another polypore that looks like a bolete. The thin, funnel-shaped velvety cap has very distinct concentric rings, ranging in colour from cinnamon to orange on a yellow ground. The underside is covered in tiny pores, the ends of the cinnamon-brown tubes. The brown flesh has a tough, corky consistency. The spores are yellow-brown.

FACT FILE

FAMILY **Hymenochaetaceae** CAP **<8cm**
HEIGHT **2–5cm** STATUS **Widespread but uncommon**

Distinctive ringed and zoned pattern on cap

Very short central stem

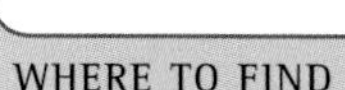

JAN FEB MAR APR MAY JUN JUL AUG SEP OCT NOV DEC

WITCHES' BUTTER

Exidia glandulosa

This rather unprepossessing fungus consists of black blobs with a gelatinous, jelly-like consistency. Like all the jelly fungi it is very variable but is generally cushion-shaped. The flesh shrinks or swells depending on the atmospheric humidity. The upperside, which is where the white spores are carried, is covered in glandular warts. The underside becomes densely covered in tiny gelatinous spines.

WHERE TO FIND

Grows on the branches of deciduous trees, especially oaks, sometimes in large clusters.

FACT FILE

FAMILY Auriculariaceae HEIGHT 1–2cm THICKNESS 1–3cm STATUS Widespread and common POSSIBLE CONFUSION Black Bulgar (p. 131) is similar but is more disc-shaped and has a black spore deposit NOTE Confusingly, Witches' Butter is also a traditional common name for the Yellow Brain (p. 79)

JAN FEB MAR APR MAY JUN **JUL AUG SEP OCT NOV** DEC

EARTHFAN

Thelephora terrestris

Very variable in appearance, but usually has fan-shaped, radiating, frilly brackets that are thin, frayed and feathery. Their surface is radially ridged and covered in short hairy fibres. The upper surface is pale brown or buff, darkening with age. The under surface is smooth to lightly wrinkled, and is brown. The brown flesh is tough and fibrous. If there is a stem, it is short and black. The spores are purple-brown.

WHERE TO FIND

Grows in large groups among mosses and fallen pine needles in coniferous woodland and on heathland.

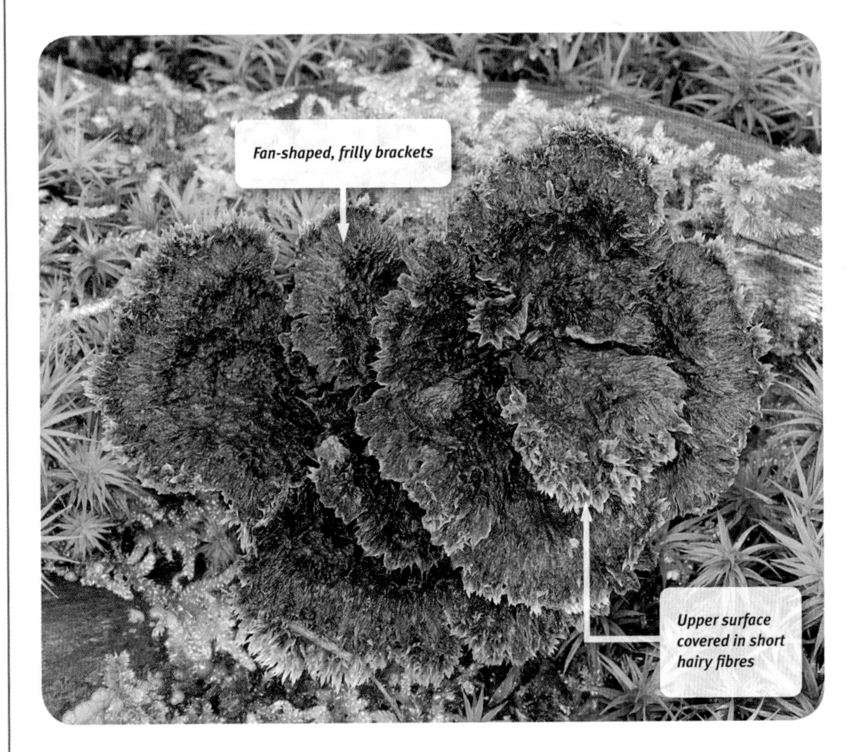

FACT FILE

FAMILY Thelephoraceae DIAMETER 5–15cm STATUS Widespread and common
POSSIBLE CONFUSION May be mistaken for the Zoned Rosette *Podoscypha multizonata*, but that is more robust and only grows under deciduous trees

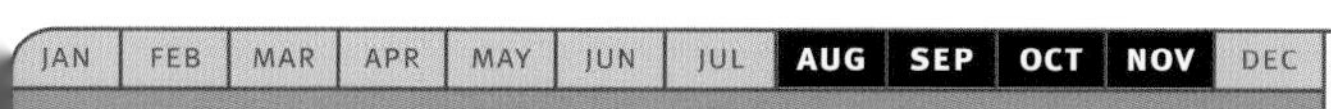

BLACK BULGAR

Bulgaria inquinans

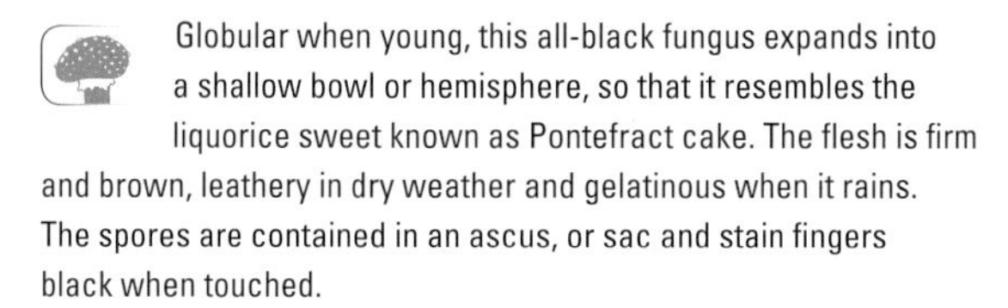

Globular when young, this all-black fungus expands into a shallow bowl or hemisphere, so that it resembles the liquorice sweet known as Pontefract cake. The flesh is firm and brown, leathery in dry weather and gelatinous when it rains. The spores are contained in an ascus, or sac and stain fingers black when touched.

WHERE TO FIND

Grows in large numbers on fallen branches of oaks, Beech *Fagus sylvatica* and Horse-chestnut *Aesculus hippocastanum*, causing them to rot.

FACT FILE

FAMILY Bulgariaceae SYNONYM Bachelor Buttons DIAMETER 1–4cm HEIGHT 1–2cm STATUS Widespread and common POSSIBLE CONFUSION May be confused with Witches' Butter (p. 129), but that species has a white, not black, spore deposit

JAN | FEB | MAR | APR | MAY | JUN | JUL | AUG | SEP | OCT | NOV | DEC

CANDLESNUFF FUNGUS

Xylaria hypoxylon

WHERE TO FIND

Grows in large numbers on dead wood of deciduous trees, especially Beech *Fagus sylvatica.*

These tiny fungi resemble nothing so much as a snuffed-out candle wick, being small, upright black twigs ending in a white tip where the asexual spores reside. The small, erect branches are cylindrical at first, eventually branching like the antlers of a Common Elk. At the same time, they flatten as the asexual spores mature. The base remains black and downy. When the fungus has dropped its asexual spores, it loses its 'antlers' and becomes thread-like and completely black, like a burnt-out match but this is the time when the sexual spores are formed.

FACT FILE

FAMILY Xylariaceae DIAMETER 2–5mm HEIGHT 3–8cm STATUS Widespread and common

JAN | FEB | MAR | APR | MAY | JUN | JUL | AUG | SEP | OCT | NOV | DEC

DEAD MAN'S FINGERS

Xylaria polymorpha

The sinister name for this fungus is well deserved as it looks like eerily distorted brownish-black or grey fingers reaching up from the ground. The outer surface is roughened from the many tiny spore-bearing cavities embedded in it, and the corky flesh is white. The spores are black.

WHERE TO FIND

Grows in clumps at the base of deciduous trees, mainly Beech *Fagus sylvatica*.

FACT FILE

FAMILY **Xylariaceae** DIAMETER **5-15mm** HEIGHT **3–8cm** STATUS **Widespread and common** POSSIBLE CONFUSION **Dead Moll's Fingers *X. longipes* is similar but the 'fingers' are more elongated**

JAN FEB MAR APR MAY **JUN JUL AUG SEP OCT NOV** DEC

BIRCH BRITTLEGILL

Russula betularum

WHERE TO FIND

Grows under birch, as its name implies, especially in damp places.

This small but beautiful brittlegill has a pale pink cap that is convex to shield-shaped. The centre of the cap is darker and becomes depressed with age, and the margin is often furrowed. The cap is slimy and shiny in wet weather, when the pink often fades to yellow or even white. The widely spaced gills and tall stem are white, as is the flesh.

FACT FILE

FAMILY Russulaceae CAP 2–5cm HEIGHT 4–8cm STATUS Widespread but uncommon
POSSIBLE CONFUSION Can be confused with Fragile Brittlegill *R. fragilis*, which has a similar habitat and is similar in size, but its cap is more purple; it is inedible. May also be mistaken for pale versions of the poisonous red-capped brittlegills such as The Sickener *R. emetica*

STINKING DAPPERLING

Lepiota cristata

The Stinking Dapperling belongs to the same family as the Parasol (p. 26) but, like all small species in the genus *Lepiota* (known in English as dapperlings), it is poisonous. All dapperlings have fibrous, scaly caps. The white cap of this species has a central dark brown umbo that flattens with age and is surrounded by brown scales that disappear towards the edge of the cap. The gills are medium spaced and are white, as are the spores. The ring is thin but may disappear entirely with age. The stem is tall and fibrous, whitish above the ring and pinkish brown below.

WHERE TO FIND

In deciduous woodland, on grass verges and in gardens.

FACT FILE

FAMILY Agaricaceae SYNONYMS Crested Lepiota, Stinking Parasol CAP 2–5cm HEIGHT 4–6cm STATUS Widespread POSSIBLE CONFUSION May be confused with other small species of *Lepiota*, all of which are poisonous

JAN FEB MAR APR MAY JUN JUL **AUG SEP OCT NOV** DEC

FLY AGARIC

Amanita muscaria

WHERE TO FIND

Mostly found under birch trees, or rarely in pinewoods.

This well-known and often depicted fungus has a bright red cap, usually covered in white warts, the remains of the universal veil that covers the whole fungus when young. The warts often form concentric patterns but may wash away completely after heavy rain, as can some of the colour in the cap, leaving it an orange colour. The cap is convex at first, flattening later, but is always rounded and lacks a central depression or umbo. The cylindrical white stem is brittle and scaly below the frilly, furrowed ring. The stem ends in a bulb surrounded by the volva – typical of all species in the genus *Amanita*.

Bright red cap, usually covered in white warts

Frilly white ring

Scaly bulb at base of stem

FACT FILE

FAMILY Amanitaceae CAP 5–15cm HEIGHT 10–20cm STATUS Widespread NOTE The species is so called because the caps were once left in saucers of milk to attract and kill flies

DEATHCAP

Amanita phalloides

The cap colour varies from almond-green (especially in young specimens) to olive-green, usually darker in the centre and fading to white at the edge. The tall, narrow stem has a floppy white striated ring about two-thirds of the way up. It is sometimes covered in greyish or ochre tufts and ends in a bulb covered with a ragged white volva, which is always present even in mature specimens – a distinctive feature. The white flesh develops a strong, sickly sweet smell when mature.

WHERE TO FIND

Associated mainly with deciduous trees such as oaks, Beech *Fagus sylvatica*, chestnuts, birches, Hazel *Corylus avellana* and Hornbeam *Carpinus betulus*; also found under pines and spruces.

LEFT: *YOUNG SPECIMEN;*
BELOW: *MATURE SPECIMEN.*

FACT FILE

FAMILY Amanitaceae CAP 5–15cm HEIGHT 8–12cm STATUS Widespread POSSIBLE CONFUSION Similar to the harmless but inedible False Deathcap *A. citrina*, in which the pale yellow or greenish cap flattens when mature and has more persistent veil remnants NOTE This species accounts for 95 per cent of all fungus poisonings in N Europe. All parts of it are poisonous, including the spores, and care must be taken to wash the hands after touching it and to keep any specimens that are collected separate from other species

JAN FEB MAR APR MAY JUN **JUL AUG SEP OCT** NOV DEC

DESTROYING ANGEL

Amanita virosa

WHERE TO FIND

Associated with various deciduous trees including birches and Beech *Fagus sylvatica*, also with spruces at high altitude.

The cap, stem, gills and flesh are all white. The cap is smooth and ovoid at first, flattening slightly in older specimens. The tall, cylindrical stem may be straight or curved, and is covered in bands of white to greyish-brown fibres arranged in a characteristic zigzag pattern. The ring is fragile and disappears completely in older specimens. The soft white flesh has an unpleasant, sickly odour.

FACT FILE

FAMILY Amanitaceae CAP 5–10cm HEIGHT 8–15cm STATUS Widespread but uncommon POSSIBLE CONFUSION Similar to the Fool's Mushroom *A. verna*, also a poisonous all-white *amanita* but found only in spring. Because all-white species – many of which are edible – are easily confused with the Destroying Angel, it is unwise for novice mushroom hunters to pick and eat them

CLUB FOOT

Ampulloclitocybe clavipes

The cap is flat with a slight umbo at first, becoming dish-shaped with a central depression. It is grey to brown, paler at the edge, and is smooth and slightly greasy in texture when wet. The margin is inrolled, gradually becoming less so. The off-white gills are deeply decurrent and quite close together. The stem is narrow at the top, thickening at the base into a club shape that may be slight to extremely pronounced. The flesh is thin and white.

WHERE TO FIND

Grows in groups in most kinds of woodland.

FACT FILE

FAMILY **Hygrophoraceae** SYNONYM *Clitocybe clavipes*
CAP **4–7cm** HEIGHT **6–8cm** STATUS **Widespread**

JAN	FEB	MAR	APR	MAY	JUN	**JUL**	**AUG**	**SEP**	**OCT**	NOV	DEC

IVORY FUNNEL

Clitocybe rivulosa

WHERE TO FIND

Grows in groups in grassland, lawns and dunes.

The greyish-white cap flattens or becomes dish-shaped in older specimens but never forms a true funnel. The texture is matt and silky, and it often has a 'frosty' appearance. The crowded white gills are attached to the stem and usually slightly decurrent. The flesh is thin and white, and has a mealy smell. The cylindrical, light brown stem is often slightly curved.

FACT FILE

FAMILY Tricholomataceae SYNONYM *Clitocybe dealbata* CAP 2–4cm HEIGHT 2–5cm STATUS Widespread but uncommon POSSIBLE CONFUSION This is one of a number of edible and poisonous all-white or off-white funnelcaps, whose similarity makes it hard for the amateur mushroom hunter to identify them with certainty. It may also be confused with the Snowy Waxcap (p. 90) and Ivory Woodwax (p. 91)

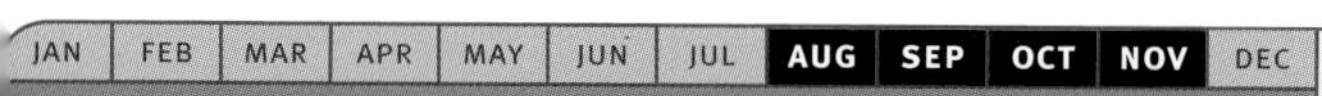

LILAC BONNET

Mycena pura

This is one of the larger members of the *Mycena* genus, which are generally small. The cap varies from lilac to brown with violet hues, and is convex at first, flattening with age. The edge of the cap is striated in older specimens. The white gills are sometimes tinged with violet, and are thick, uneven and widely spaced. The stem is sturdy, narrowing slightly at the top. It is a similar colour to the cap and silky or fibrillose. It has a distinctive radish-like smell.

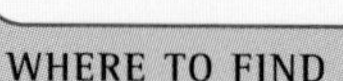

On leaf litter in mixed woodlands.

FACT FILE

FAMILY Mycenaceae CAP 2–5cm HEIGHT 4–7cm STATUS Widespread POSSIBLE CONFUSION May be confused with other purple-capped species, such as the Amethyst Deceiver (p. 42) or Wood Blewit (p. 36) NOTE In the variety *M. pura* var. *rosea* the cap is pink

JAN	FEB	MAR	APR	MAY	JUN	JUL	**AUG**	**SEP**	**OCT**	**NOV**	**DEC**

LIVID PINKGILL

Entoloma sinuatum

WHERE TO FIND

Grows in rings or small groups, sometimes joining together at the base in clumps, under deciduous trees.

The entolomas have pink gills and most are poisonous. In the Livid Pinkgill, the hemispherical cap is dirty cream to leaden grey and remains inrolled for a long time. The white flesh is thick below the centre of the cap. The gills are uneven and widely spaced, turning from yellow to flesh-coloured as the spores mature. The spores are pink. The white stem is thick, slightly swollen at the base and covered in short fibrils; it turns grey with age.

FACT FILE

FAMILY Entolomataceae SYNONYMS Lead Poisoner, Leaden Pinkgill CAP 5–20cm HEIGHT 6–12cm STATUS Widespread and common POSSIBLE CONFUSION The Clouded Funnel *Clitocybe nebularis* is similar, but has white spores and no pink tinge to the gills

BROWN ROLLRIM

Paxillus involutus

The rollrims are so named as their caps remain inrolled into maturity. All members of the genus are poisonous. In the Brown Rollrim, the brown to reddish-brown cap is thick and fleshy. It has a shallow depression in the centre when older and is irregularly lobed. The flesh is thick, soft and yellowish, turning brown on contact with the air. The gills are cream-coloured at first, eventually becoming splashed with rusty brown from the brown spores, and run down the stem. The stem is brownish, and often very short and eccentric.

WHERE TO FIND

Under deciduous and coniferous trees in damp grassland and parks, and on grass verges.

FACT FILE

FAMILY Paxillaceae CAP 5–15cm HEIGHT 4–10cm
STATUS Widespread and extremely common

JAN FEB MAR APR MAY JUN **JUL AUG SEP OCT NOV** DEC

OYSTER ROLLRIM

Tapinella panuoides

WHERE TO FIND

Grows in groups on decayed coniferous wood.

The fan- or ear-shaped cap is irregularly lobed and strongly inrolled even into maturity. It is yellow-brown to ochre, velvety in texture but becoming leathery with age. The stem is often eccentric and is part of the cap, being extremely short or even missing altogether. The gills are pale yellow and very thin. The spores are brown.

FACT FILE

FAMILY Tapinellaceae SYNONYM *Paxillus panuoides*
CAP 3–6cm STATUS Widespread but uncommon

FUNERAL BELL

Galerina marginata

The shiny, convex cap can be various shades of brown or ochre, paler in dry weather. It is very thin at the edge, such that the straight, crowded gills show through it. The gills are fawn to brown, darkening as the brown spores ripen. The most distinctive feature is the long stem, which is cylindrical and quite slender, thickening slightly towards the base. It is white but covered in darker fibrils, these greyish or brown. The remains of a ring may be seen in the top third of the stem. The flesh is yellowish under the cap but brown in the stem. The mushroom smells strongly of meal.

Long stem with remains of ring

WHERE TO FIND

Almost always found in clusters on rotting wood, both deciduous and coniferous.

FACT FILE

FAMILY Hymenogastraceae SYNONYMS Deadly Galerina, Autumn Skullcap CAP 2–7cm HEIGHT 4–8cm STATUS Widespread POSSIBLE CONFUSION Could be confused with edible brown-capped species such as the Honey Fungus *Armillaria mellea* and Sheathed Woodtuft (p. 49) NOTE Before 2001, four other galerinas were thought to be separate species; DNA sequencing has since shown these all to be *G. marginata*

Grows in clusters

Two-toned cap, very thin at edge

JAN	FEB	MAR	APR	MAY	JUN	JUL	**AUG**	**SEP**	**OCT**	**NOV**	DEC

POISONPIE

Hebeloma crustuliniforme

WHERE TO FIND

Grows in large groups on the ground in mixed woodlands.

The cream to fawn cap is hemispherical at first, flattening out with a wide, shallow central umbo. The cap becomes sticky when wet. The gills are crowded and flesh-coloured. The white flesh is thick and firm, and smells strongly of radishes. The sturdy stem is covered in tiny white flakes. The spores are brown.

FACT FILE

FAMILY Hymenogastraceae CAP 5–10cm HEIGHT 5–10cm
STATUS Widespread and common NOTE This fungus causes vomiting and diarrhoea rather than death, so some authorities merely list it as 'indigestible'

JAN | FEB | MAR | APR | MAY | JUN | **JUL** | **AUG** | **SEP** | **OCT** | NOV | DEC

SPLIT FIBRECAP

Inocybe rimosa

All the members of the genus *Inocybe* are poisonous or suspect. The cap of this species is straw-coloured to light brown, and is distinctive in being covered from the centre to the edge in long brown fibres. It is hemispherical at first, becoming flatter with age but always with a central umbo. As with many other members of the genus, the cap splits virtually in half as the fungus ages. The gills are yellowish green, edged with white, and darken with age as the brown spores mature. The stem is quite sturdy, white or reddish, and covered in small fluffy scales that give it a velvety look. There is no ring.

WHERE TO FIND

On well-drained sandy or limestone soil in deciduous woods, on grass verges and in clearings.

FACT FILE

FAMILY Inocybaceae SYNONYMS Silken-haired Inocybe, *Inocybe fastigiata*
CAP 3–8cm HEIGHT 5–10cm STATUS Widespread but uncommon

JAN FEB MAR APR MAY JUN **JUL AUG SEP OCT** NOV DEC

WHITE FIBRECAP

Inocybe geophylla

WHERE TO FIND

Under deciduous trees, often in large numbers.

The white cap is conical with a central umbo that is occasionally ochre-coloured. The surface is smooth and silky, sticky when wet. The flesh is white or cream and has an unpleasant smell. As with many other members of the genus, the cap virtually splits in half as the fungus ages. The crowded gills are off-white or beige, darkening with age as the brown spores mature. The white stem is long and thin, swelling into a small bulb at the base. There is no ring.

FACT FILE

FAMILY Inocybaceae CAP 1–3cm HEIGHT 2–5cm STATUS Widespread and common POSSIBLE CONFUSION Lilac Leg Fibrecap *I. griseolilacina* is similar, with a lilac-tinged brown cap; it grows on nitrate-rich soil in deciduous woodland NOTE There is a lilac-capped variety, Lilac Fibrecap *I. geophylla* var. *lilacina*, also poisonous

BROWN MOTTLEGILL

Panaeolina foenisecii

The cap is hemispherical, broadening with age but never becoming completely flat. It is dark brown when fresh or moist, drying much paler from the centre out. The tall stem is light brown and hollow, and covered in white powder when young. The flesh is thin and brown. The pale brown gills are broad, have a lighter edge and become mottled as the spores develop. The spores are black.

WHERE TO FIND

Grows at hay-making time in all types of grassland, including meadows, borders, parks and lawns.

FACT FILE

FAMILY Bolbitiaceae SYNONYMS *Panaeolus foenisecii*, Haymaker, Brown Hay Cap, Mower's Mushroom CAP 2–3cm HEIGHT 4–7cm STATUS Widespread and common

JAN FEB MAR APR MAY JUN **JUL AUG SEP OCT NOV** DEC

COMMON RUSTGILL

Gymnopilus penetrans

WHERE TO FIND

Grows in isolation or in small groups on rotting conifer branches and conifer cones.

The bright orange to yellow-orange cap is convex, expanding and flattening with age. The flesh is whitish and has no smell. The crowded gills are sulphur-yellow at first, turning rusty brown, with darker spots, as the brown spores mature. The long yellowish stem is often curved and thickens at the base, which is often covered in white down.

FACT FILE

FAMILY Strophariaceae CAP 3–8cm
HEIGHT 3–6cm STATUS Widespread and common
POSSIBLE CONFUSION The related Spectacular Rustgill (p. 151) is similar in colour, but is larger and more striking, and grows only on deciduous trees

JAN FEB MAR APR MAY JUN **JUL AUG SEP OCT NOV** DEC

SPECTACULAR RUSTGILL

Gymnopilus junonius

The thick golden-brown cap is covered in concolorous fibrous scales, becoming streaked as it ages. The gills are orange at first, turning rusty brown as the brown spores mature. The stem is yellowish, sometimes swollen towards the base and has a prominent ring; it is also yellow but becomes stained brown from the spores.

WHERE TO FIND

On the branches, stumps and base of decaying deciduous trees.

FACT FILE

FAMILY Strophariaceae
SYNONYMS Fiery Agaric, Laughing Jim, *Pholiota spectabilis*, *Gymnopilus spectabilis*
CAP 5–15cm
HEIGHT 5–15cm
STATUS Widespread and common

JAN FEB MAR **APR MAY JUN JUL AUG SEP OCT NOV** DEC

SULPHUR TUFT

Hypholoma fasciculare

WHERE TO FIND

Grows in large tufts on the dead wood of deciduous and coniferous trees.

The smooth cap is hemispherical at first, soon expanding to a shallow bowl. It is ochre in the centre and bright yellow at the edge. The cap margin may have shreds of the thin veil, or cortina, hanging from it. The gills are bright lemon-yellow, turning greenish as the purple-brown spores ripen. The long, bright yellow stem is cylindrical and quite slender, and sometimes bears the faint signs of a dark brown ring. It is often curved to ensure the cap is parallel to the ground for spore dispersal. The flesh is yellowish under the cap but brown in the stem.

FACT FILE

FAMILY Strophariaceae

CAP 2–7cm HEIGHT 4–10cm

STATUS Widespread and common

POSSIBLE CONFUSION The Sheathed Woodtuft (p. 49) and Honey Fungus *Armillaria mellea*, both edible, are similar but neither has the greenish tint to the gills or yellow stem of this species

Hemispherical cap is ochre in the centre, yellow at the edge

Grows in large tufts

Gills and stem yellow, sometimes with remains of brown ring

JAN | FEB | MAR | APR | MAY | JUN | JUL | **AUG** | **SEP** | **OCT** | **NOV** | DEC

SHAGGY SCALYCAP

Pholiota squarrosa

The pale yellow to brown cap is egg-shaped at first, becoming hemispherical but never completely flattening. It is covered in dark brown scales. The flesh is white, thick and fibrous, and has an unpleasant smell. The gills are pale yellow and crowded, turning rust-coloured as the purple-brown spores ripen. The long, sinuous stem is pale yellow but thickly covered in brown scales below the membranous ring.

WHERE TO FIND

Grows in clumps on wood of deciduous trees, especially at the base of living trees.

FACT FILE

FAMILY Strophariaceae CAP 5–12cm HEIGHT 6–15cm STATUS Widespread POSSIBLE CONFUSION The Golden Scalycap (p. 50) is similar but has a slimy cap and is less shaggy

JAN FEB MAR APR MAY **JUN JUL AUG SEP OCT NOV** DEC

YELLOW STAINER

Agaricus xanthodermus

WHERE TO FIND

On woodland edges, parks and lawns.

The white cap is hemispherical at first, flattening with age and bruising bright yellow at the margin. As in all members of the genus, the cap peels easily. The remains of the veil form a thick ring on the tall white stem, which stains bright yellow at its base when cut or scraped – a key distinguishing character. The thick flesh is white and has an unpleasant inky smell – another important characteristic. The gills are crowded, light pink at first and darkening to brownish black as the purple-brown spores ripen.

FACT FILE

FAMILY Agaricaceae SYNONYM *Psalliota xanthoderma* CAP 7–15cm HEIGHT 10–15cm STATUS Widespread and common POSSIBLE CONFUSION Similar to other members of the genus, especially the Field Mushroom (p. 52) NOTE Accounts for the greatest number of mushroom poisonings in the UK, although some people are not affected by it

JAN | FEB | MAR | APR | MAY | JUN | **JUL** | **AUG** | **SEP** | **OCT** | **NOV** | DEC

COMMON INKCAP

Coprinopsis atramentaria

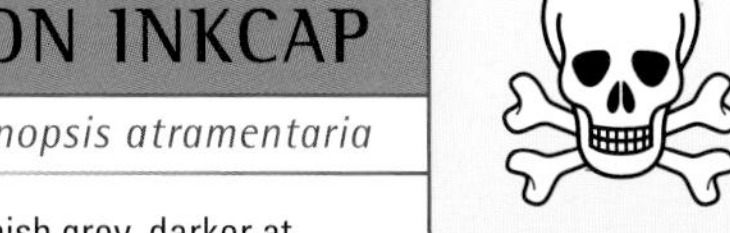

The ovoid cap is silvery grey to brownish grey, darker at the top. It is striated and silky, and expands into an umbrella shape. The margin splits and becomes ragged in older specimens as it starts to deliquesce. The gills are off-white when young, darkening as the black spores mature. The thin brown flesh has a pleasant taste and smell. The sturdy white stem does not deliquesce.

WHERE TO FIND

Grows in dense clusters that may be welded together at the base of the stem, on rotting wood that is usually buried.

FACT FILE

FAMILY Psathyrellaceae SYNONYM *Coprinus atramenarius* CAP 3–7cm HEIGHT 5–15cm STATUS Widespread and common NOTE When eaten with alcohol it causes nausea, vomiting and heart palpitations, and so was once used as an aversion therapy treatment for alcoholics. The symptoms persist for days after ingestion

JAN	FEB	MAR	APR	MAY	JUN	**JUL**	**AUG**	**SEP**	**OCT**	NOV	DEC

COMMON EARTHBALL

Scleroderma citrinum

Has pale ochre skin covered in prominent, coarse, angular brownish scales. The outer skin is thick, tough and coarse, eventually tearing open at maturity. The spore mass inside is white, then pink and eventually black, marbled with white veins. It is attached to the soil by multiple white mycelial cords.

WHERE TO FIND

Usually grows in groups on siliceous soil among deciduous trees on heathland and in grassland.

FACT FILE

FAMILY **Sclerodermataceae** SYNONYMS *Scleroderma aurantium*, *Scleroderma vulgare*, **Pigskin Poison Puffball** DIAMETER **4–12cm** STATUS **Widespread and common** POSSIBLE CONFUSION **May be mistaken for a small puffball (pp. 65 & 67), but when cut open reveals its thick skin and black interior**

ERGOT

Claviceps purpurea

Ergot is an ascomycete, a fungus that carries its spores in a sac called an ascus. It forms structures known as sclerotia that are long, purple and bean-shaped, and protrude from among the ears of Rye. They emerge from a mass of mycelium, which invades the ear and eventually destroys it. The sclerotia can overwinter and fruit the following year when the Rye is ripening.

WHERE TO FIND

Parasitic on many grasses such as Rye *Secale cereale*.

FACT FILE

FAMILY Clavicipitaceae HEIGHT 3–10mm STATUS Widespread and common NOTE In the past, Ergot was responsible for many poisonings; it is now used medicinally as a vasoconstrictor

FURTHER INFORMATION

There are huge numbers of books on fungi illustrated with photographs and coloured illustrations for identification. Readers are advised to acquire recent publications as the names of fungi, both common and scientific, change frequently. For those wishing to go deeper into the subject, monographs are recommended.

References and Further Reading

The following are a mixture of comprehensive field guides and books explaining the place of fungi in the world.

Bacon, J. (2010) *A Naturalist's Guide to the Mushrooms and Other Fungi of Britain & Northern Europe*. John Beaufoy Publishing.

Buczacki, S. (2012) *Mushrooms and Toadstools of Britain and Europe*. HarperCollins.

Buczacki, S. (2012) *Collins Fungi Guide*. HarperCollins.

Harding, P. (2006) *Mushroom Hunting*, Need to Know Series. HarperCollins.

Harding, P. (2008) *Collins Mushroom Miscellany*. HarperCollins.

Harding, P., Lyon, T. & Tomblin, G. (1996) *How to Identify Edible Mushrooms*. HarperCollins.

Jordan, Michael (1995) *The Encyclopedia of Fungi of Britain and Europe*. David & Charles.

Kavaler, Lucy (2007) *Mushrooms, Molds, and Miracles*. iUniverse.Knudsen, H. & Vesterholt, J. (2008) *Fungi nordica*, 2nd edition. Nordsvamp.

Kühner, R. & Romagnesi, H. (1974) *Flore analytique des champignons supérieurs*. Masson.

Large, E.C. (1960) *The Advance of the Fungi*. Jonathan Cape.

Pegler, D. (2001) *Mushrooms & Toadstools of Britain and Europe*. Kingfisher.

Roper, A. (2009) *Mushroom Magick*. Abrams.

Sterry, P. & Hughes, B. (2009) *Collins Complete Guide to British Mushrooms and Toadstools*. HarperCollins.

Fungal Identification

In view of the danger of making mistakes, it is a very good idea for novices to attend identification workshops. These are held all over the country. Consult the website of the British Mycological Society, http://www.britmycolsoc.org.uk/, which has lots of information about local groups and activities for children. For private courses on fungus identification held all over the country, visit the website http://www.hotcourses.com/uk-courses/Fungi-Identification-courses/hc2_browse.

The website of the European Mycological Association, http://www.euromould.org/links/socs.htm, has details of mycological societies all over the world.

The British Mycological Society's quarterly publication *Field Mycology* is a great help in identifying rare species.

INDEX

Tick boxes are included next to the main English name of each species so you can mark off species that you have seen.